THE NEW
PAPER QUILLING

THE NEW
PAPER QUILLING

BY MOLLY SMITH CHRISTENSEN

LARK
CRAFTS

A Division of Sterling Publishing Co., Inc.
New York / London

The Library of Congress has cataloged the hardcover edition as follows:

Smith Christensen, Molly, 1953-
 The new paper quilling : creative techniques for
scrapbooks, cards, home accents & more / Molly Smith
Christensen.
     p. cm.
 Includes index.
 ISBN 1-57990-691-5 (hardcover)
 1. Paper quillwork. I. Title.
TT870.S5738 2006
745.54--dc22
                                    2005032344

10 9 8 7 6 5 4 3 2 1

Published by Lark Books, A Division of
Sterling Publishing Co., Inc.
387 Park Avenue South, New York, N.Y. 10016

First Paperback Edition 2010
Text © 2006, Molly Smith Christensen
Illustrations © 2006, Lark Books, A Division of Sterling Publishing Co., Inc.;
unless otherwise specified
Illustrations © 2006, Lark Books, A Division of Sterling Publishing Co., Inc.;
unless otherwise specified

Lyrics to "Midnight at the Oasis," on page 73, © 1973, 1974 Space Potato Music
Ltd. (ASCAP). All rights reserved. Used by permission of publisher.

Distributed in Canada by Sterling Publishing,
c/o Canadian Manda Group, 165 Dufferin Street
Toronto, Ontario, Canada M6K 3H6

Distributed in the United Kingdom by GMC Distribution Services,
Castle Place, 166 High Street, Lewes, East Sussex, England BN7 1XU

Distributed in Australia by Capricorn Link (Australia) Pty Ltd.,
P.O. Box 704, Windsor, NSW 2756 Australia

If you have questions or comments about this book, please contact:
Lark Books
67 Broadway
Asheville, NC 28801
(828) 253-0467

Manufactured in China

ISBN-13: 978-1-57990-691-7 (hardcover) 978-1-60059-556-1 (paperback)

For information about custom editions, special sales, premium and corporate
purchases, please contact Sterling Special Sales Department at 800-805-5489
or specialsales@sterlingpub.com.

For information about desk and examination copies available to college and uni-
versity professors, requests must be submitted to academic@larkbooks.com.
Our complete policy can be found at www.larkbooks.com.

Editor:

Terry Taylor

Art Directors:

Megan Kirby, Dana Irwin

Cover Designer:

Barbara Zaretsky

Associate Editor:

Nathalie Mornu

Assistant Art Director:

Lance Wille

Art Production Assistants:

Jeff Hamilton, Bradley Norris

Copy Editor:

Kathy Sheldon

Editorial Assistance:

Delores Gosnell

Editorial Intern:

David Squires

Art Interns:

Nathan Schulman, Emily Kepley

Illustrator:

Orrin Lundgren

Photographer:

Steve Mann

CONTENTS

INTRODUCTION

Are you a paper crafter looking for new ways to play with paper? Or are you a quiller looking for new techniques, projects, and patterns? Whether you're a beginner or an expert—*The New Paper Quilling* is the book for you.

Simply put, quilling, also known as paper filigree, involves rolling, scrolling, shaping, or fringing of narrow strips of paper to create lovely designs. The art of quilling has been traced to European monasteries of the 15th century, but the actual creation of the art may date back two centuries earlier. It's thought that feather quills were originally used to roll the paper strips. The revival of quilling in recent years is one of the highlights of the popularity of paper crafts.

Quilling is easy to learn and doesn't require a large investment in specialized tools. To start, all you need are paper strips, a corsage pin, and craft glue. Many of the materials and supplies are simple household items or basic craft tools you already own. I'll help you assemble a Basic Quilling Tool Kit before you start any project. You'll have everything you need at hand and can dive right in.

I've been quilling for more than 25 years and have come up with 30 project designs that range from cute and easy to sophisticated and challenging. In many projects you'll use only one or two simple shapes. Many of the projects can be completed in one day or just a few hours. You'll be surprised how quickly you can make a project that you'll be proud of.

Flowers and plants are always favorite themes with quillers so there are plenty of these throughout the book—from big bold designs like the Funky Faux Flowers on page 70 to a delicate traditional project like Bouquetière on page 94. But flowers and plants aren't all you have to choose from.

If you're looking for ways to perk up your scrapbooking, try quilling a word or phrase with one of the three alphabets I've created. For a one-of-a-kind home accent, quill yourself a Très Chic Trio of dresses and frame them for your walls. Make a veritable produce stand of colorful magnets to dress up your refrigerator. Discover ways to make holidays and special occasions even more memorable with simple quilled decorations.

First, read through the Basics section. You'll find step-by-step instructions and illustrations for a variety of traditional quilling shapes and be introduced to new techniques to use such as crimping paper strips, and shading quilled shapes with chalk or ink. Throughout the book I'll give you tips that I've learned over the years (sometimes the hard way!)—simple things that will save you time and eliminate unnecessary steps.

Then flip through the book and see what captures your interest. Is it that charming bouquet of embossed tulips, or the dazzling, colorful mobile? Feel free to put your own individual stamp on any of the projects by using different colors of paper or adding a decorative technique you like. Experiment with a variety of papers—textured, patterned, different weights; you might even try using metal foils. Adjust the size of a

pattern to suit your needs. Make one object from a multi-piece project or make them all. Use this book as a guide—if you want a blue flower, for goodness sakes, make a blue flower!

If you're a complete beginner—practice, practice, practice! In a short period of time all of your efforts will fall into place and your shapes will be perfect. Strive for perfection, but accept that a little imperfection adds character to your piece. After all, it's handcrafted.

If you get overwhelmed while quilling a large project, set it aside for another day or time. Then, make just one flower and embellish a small gift tag, or shape a single quilled initial and glue it to a pretty little box.

Accomplishing small projects always gives me a sense of satisfaction, refuels my creativity, and gives me a nudge to attempt or complete the bigger tasks. I always set some time aside to be creative in simple ways. You should too. Happy quilling!

QUILLING BASICS

Have you ever rolled a corner of a page in a book or magazine? Or rolled up a dollar bill, receipt, or ticket stub? If you have, then you can quill. Anyone can learn to quill with a corsage pin, a few narrow strips of paper, and a dab of glue. Paper quilling is an inexpensive and popular craft that allows you, in very little time, to create a wide variety of decorative items.

TOOLS AND SUPPLIES

Before you start, you'll need to assemble a few tools and supplies to put together a basic quilling tool kit. Many of these are items you may already have on hand or can purchase inexpensively. Each project in this book lists the basic quilling tool kit as the first item under What You Need. It may not be necessary to have every item in the tool kit when you first start quilling, but each item has a specific use that will help to simplify the process of quilling.

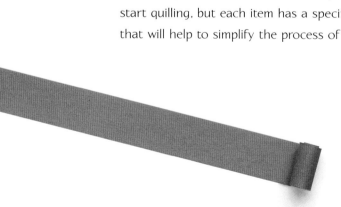

Basic Quilling Tool Kit

Needle quilling tool
Slotted quilling tool
Basic craft glue
All-purpose craft glue
Toothpicks
Waxed paper
Clear sheets of acetate
Fine-point, bent-nose tweezers
Scissors
Ruler
Tracing paper and pencil
Straight pins
Work surface

Quilling Tools

The first quillers may have used the quills of feathers to roll strips of paper torn from books. Modern quillers have it a bit easier, since most use a slotted quilling tool, a needle tool, or a corsage pin, and can buy precut paper. While the corsage pin is the more traditional quilling tool, the slotted quilling tool and the needle tool (which both have their needle ends set into handles) are easier to use and therefore a good choice for the beginner.

A slotted tool has a narrow slot at the end of its needle that holds the quilling paper so it won't slip off the tool as you start rolling. But it can be a bit tricky at first to place the strip in the slot properly. If the end of the strip is placed too far into the slot and sticks out past it, the paper will bend and make a tag in the center of your quilled circle. With just a little practice, you should be able to thread your strip so the slotted tool causes only a slight, barely visible bend at the end of the paper.

In addition to making it easier to roll tight circles, the slotted tool is used to make fringed flowers, folded roses, and bullets. You can use the butt of the handle to smooth out the top of tight circles, and the handle itself can serve as a handy 1/4-inch dowel.

The needle on a needle tool has a tapered tip; it's slightly larger in circumference and longer

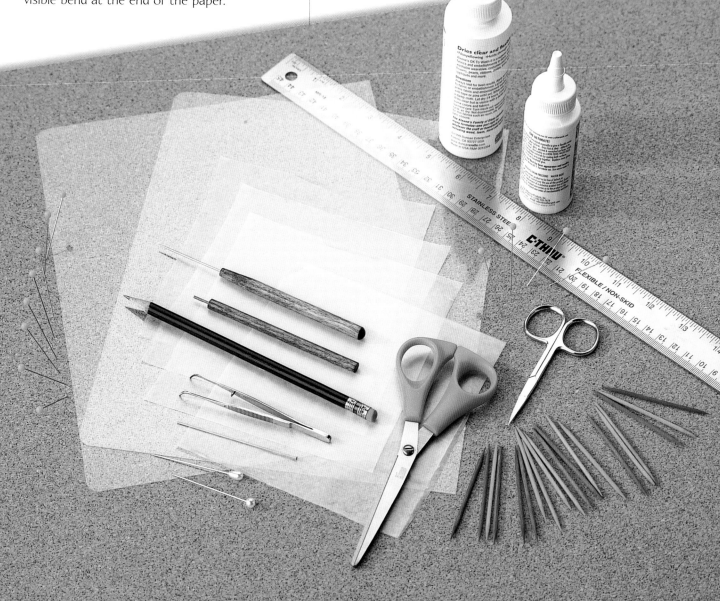

than a corsage pin, so it's easier to control when you're rolling paper. The long handle makes the tool comfortable to use, and the needle (which doesn't use a slot to hold the paper) helps you to make small, uniform centers in your rolls—the mark of well-done quilling.

To roll paper with a needle tool or a corsage pin, place the end of the paper against your index finger and place the quilling tool on the end of the paper. Press the end of the paper around the tool with your thumb and roll the paper without turning the tool. Keep the edges even as you roll. If it's difficult to get the paper to start around the tool, slightly moisten the end of the paper strip and try again.

Although quilling is a very easy technique to learn, becoming proficient with a quilling tool can take a bit of practice. No matter which tool you select—a corsage pin, the slotted tool, or the needle tool—give yourself a little time to practice rolling. Before you know it, you'll be making uniform rolls.

Glues

The most important thing to remember about using glue is that only a small amount is needed—no matter how perfectly your pieces are quilled, too much glue will ruin your project.

Your quilling kit should always include white, water-based craft or hobby glue that dries clear and is recommended for work with paper. You may also want to have a thicker, all-purpose craft glue that dries clear and can be used on glass, plastics, metal, wood, and other difficult-to-glue surfaces. As you gain experience as a quiller, you may decide to use only this type of glue. Experiment and use what works best for you.

Toothpicks

Round wooden toothpicks are used in several projects as a small dowel for rolling and shaping, and they can even be used as a needle tool—by children as well as adults. Just about any kind of toothpick (plastic or wooden, round or square) will make it easy to apply glue to paper shapes and pattern pieces. Plastic food picks with sharp points are perfect for applying small amounts of glue as well.

Waxed Paper

Waxed paper is a handy material with many uses. Place sheets over a work surface and refresh with a new sheet as necessary. Just remember to apply only small amounts of glue to your pieces—too much glue on the bottom of your pieces will cause them to stick to the waxed paper. To make cleanup easy, use it when painting strips of paper so the paint won't stick to your work surface. If you're using a pattern, you can lay the waxed paper right over the pattern and work, or substitute the waxed paper for tracing paper and trace a pattern onto the waxed paper first. (The result won't be as easy to see as when using tracing paper, so you'll need to place the waxed paper over a dark background.) Keep small squares of waxed paper at your work area and use them to hold small globs of glue.

Bent-Nose Tweezers

Tweezers are indispensable tools when you're adding tiny items such as pearls or rhinestones to your pieces or assembling shapes into a pattern. Any style of tweezers can be used, but fine-point, bent-nose tweezers are the easiest. The curved tips allow you to see your work better when assembling, and they position small pieces precisely in tight spots. You can also use tweezers to remove coils from your designer work board.

Scissors

Sharp craft scissors have many uses. Feel free to use your favorite paper scissors, but you'll probably want to use other types too. Decorative-edge, micro-tip, and curved scissors are helpful, so try to keep several sizes and types close by. Small, fine, straight-blade scissors are best for intricate fringing. Use your dull scissors to cut metal, plastic, and thick paper.

Ruler

A 12- or 18-inch ruler is essential. Any type of ruler will work, but a stainless-steel ruler with a cork backing is suggested since it's easy to cut against with a craft knife or rotary cutter and the cork back prevents slipping.

Tracing Paper and Pencil

The easiest way to make a working pattern from any book is to photocopy the page. If you don't have a photocopier (or access to one), use thin, translucent tracing paper (or waxed paper) and a pencil to transfer your patterns. Place the traced pieces under your acetate cover. Although it's possible to place a piece of acetate over a book page, it's not very practical.

Straight Pins

Use straight pins to hold quilled shapes in place over a pattern on your work board as you glue the shapes together. If a straight pin is at least 1 1/4 inches in length, it can be used in a pinch as a quilling tool to roll short strips or to make very small shapes with teeny-tiny centers—a must for quilling miniatures. Use straight pins to attach acetate or other materials to your work board and to apply glue.

Acetate

You'll do much of your quilling on a clear sheet of acetate (the material commonly used to make transparencies that's similar to page protectors, dividers, and report covers). Acetate works well because its surface offers stability for quilled shapes and pieces as they're being made, but—once the glue on your piece has dried—it allows you to easily pry off the piece with the tip of a quilling tool. A sheet of acetate is needed when applying a glue-backing (see page 27). Hold acetate in place over your work board with straight pins or tape. A smaller piece can be used in lieu of waxed paper to hold globs of glue. The dried glue is easily removed, and the acetate can be washed and used repeatedly.

Work Surfaces

Just about any flat surface covered with a sheet of waxed paper will work for quilling: You can work at a desk, on a tabletop, or sitting in your favorite chair with a large book on your lap. A TV tray makes a perfect portable quilling station. Trays with short legs made for children can be placed on your lap and will allow you to work in any comfortable spot. You'll find them at yard sales, large discount stores, or perhaps in a family member's garage.

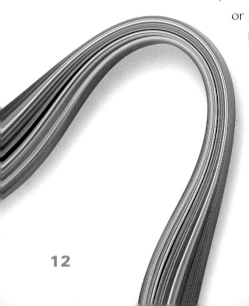

As you gain experience in quilling, you may want to use a more professional work board. A cork work board has many benefits.

You can lay graph paper or patterns on the surface and then cover them with a sheet of acetate held down with straight pins or tape. Work boards are portable, so they're easy to put away without disturbing an unfinished piece. If you have two or more work boards, you can continue quilling on one while large assembled pieces are drying on another.

Self-healing cork work boards with various paper templates can be purchased at most craft supply stores and online. However, you can make your own easily with just a few supplies. Cork comes in sheets and rolls of various sizes and can be purchased at craft and home improvement stores. Make your work board any size you like, but figure on using a 1/4-inch-thick piece of cork that's at least 8 x 10 inches (two pieces can be glued together to make a thicker board). Simply cover the cork with a sheet of white or graph paper, place a sheet of clear acetate on top, and secure it to the board with straight pins across the top and one pin on each side, and you've got a work board. (Extra-thick acetate can be secured with tape at the top and sides instead.)

On page 123, you'll find a full-size template for a work board that's perfect for quilling and has many helpful features. To use it, simply enlarge and photocopy the template onto a clear sheet of printer-ready acetate. The circles will help you measure the diameters of quilled loose cir-

cles as specified in project instructions. The ruler helps to quickly measure lengths of paper. Graph paper gives you an estimate of the size of work at a glance.

PAPERS

While any and all types of paper can be used for quilling, precut, packaged quilling strips are the most convenient and economical to purchase. The strips come in various widths, lengths, colors, and textures. They can be purchased at craft supply stores and online.

Packaged Quilling Paper

Precut and packaged quilling strips come in just about every color and shade and in four widths: narrow ($1/16$ inch), standard ($1/8$ inch), wide ($1/4$ inch), and extra wide ($3/8$ inch). You can also purchase precut specialty strips in widths of $1/2$ inch, $3/4$ inch, and 1 inch. Quilling strips range from 17 to 25 inches in length, depending on the manufacturer. In addition to solid colors (includ-

ing metallic gold and silver), specialty quilling paper is available pearlized, speckled, two-toned, with gilded edges, and in graduated colors.

Decorative Papers

Scrapbook paper—every kind of paper used in making scrapbooks—can be used to quill. While the two-sided prints and colors work best, those with white on one side can be chalked, painted, inked, or left with one side blank.

Vellum makes beautiful paper strips, creases and folds easily, and is best for dry embossing. However, when using vellum, you need to wait longer for the glue to dry, and you'll have to hide glued parts when assembling since the glue will show through the vellum.

Wrapping paper is more useful than you might think. You can make gorgeous quilled bows from holiday wrapping paper and matching gift tags or cards from scrap pieces. Heavier-weight wrapping paper is best for crimping. Don't throw away the last bit of paper on a roll—experiment and use it for quilling!

Handmade and textured papers make unique quilling strips. The textures and fibers are more eye-catching if you use wider strips. And the effect is enhanced if crimped first. Test several samples for ease of rolling, gluing, and overall result.

Card stock is used in many of this book's projects, usually crimped before being quilled. It's available in a variety of colors and sizes. It's also inexpensive and is often on sale in craft stores. Crimped card stock releases evenly and makes perfectly centered coils.

Standard, colored copying paper has been used for years to make quilling strips. The weight of this paper is comparable to precut quilling strips. Although it's not available in as many colors as other papers, it can be purchased in multicolor packages at a local office supply store. This is the favorite paper among quillers who make their own strips and is the least expensive to purchase.

Making Your Own Quilling Strips

If you don't have access to prepackaged quilling strips and want to start quilling right away, there are three ways to create your own paper strips for quilling.

Use a craft knife or a rotary cutter to cut strips by hand. For accuracy, use a ruler and measure and mark the widths with a pencil. This is a quick and easy way to cut wide strips. Of course, you can cut all widths of paper strips with a large pair of scissors—this works best with sharp scissors that have ergonomic handles.

You can use a paper trimmer to make precise strips $\frac{1}{8}$ inch and wider. A guillotine-type paper cutter can be used if it has a guard at the edge to hold the paper down and keep it from shifting so the strips will be even and accurate.

A paper shredder provides an easy and fast way to make strips for quilling. Quilling strips $\frac{1}{8}$ and $\frac{1}{4}$ inch in width can be created following the instructions on page 17.

Optional Tools

As you complete various projects in this book, you may find that you need tools other than those in the Basic Quilling Tool Kit. These tools usually will make the quilling easier or quicker or will create some special effect. Many more quilling tools are on the market than are featured here. While some of these also make quilling easier and faster, others are nothing more than a "must-have" for those who love gadgets. What follows is a list of additional tools—some you may find you can't live without, and some that you probably can.

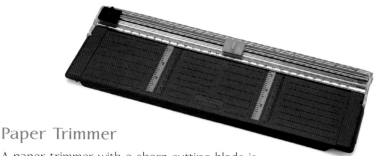

Optional Tool Kit

Paper crimper
Paper trimmer
Dowels
Fine-tip glue bottle
Decoupage scissors
Dry-embossing tool
Metal pins (for spirals)
Designer work board
Fringing tool
Paper shredder
Craft knife
Rotary cutter
Hand punches

Paper Crimper

A paper crimper makes a "corrugated" effect. Several sizes and styles are available in craft stores. The larger crimper is easy to use and can handle sheets up to 9 inches wide. It's good for crimping 1/4-inch and wider paper, several pieces at a time. A smaller crimper made specifically for crimping 1/8-inch and narrower paper strips can be purchased at quilling supply stores online.

Paper Trimmer

A paper trimmer with a sharp cutting blade is highly recommended for making the projects in this book. Many trimmers are on the market, ranging from an inexpensive standard 12-inch trimmer with a straight blade to a more costly 12-inch trimmer with a rotary blade, swing-out ruler, and face plate with 1/8-inch guidelines—perfect for making your own paper strips.

Dowels

Dowels are used with quilling to shape a quilled piece into various configurations. Kitchen tool handles, pen or marker barrels, glue sticks, empty prescription bottles, and the handles of quilling tools can all serve as dowels and aid you in shaping quilled pieces. Keeping several sizes of dowels nearby will allow you to shape with ease.

Fine-Tip Glue Bottle

While not absolutely necessary, a fine-tip glue bottle will prove very convenient when quilling. Your glue won't dry out quickly, it'll be readily available at your side, and it will be easy to dispense a precise amount of glue—you are in control. A metal .5 mm tip bottle is ideal for quilling. While you work, keep the bottle turned upside down in a small glass container (a candle votive works well). A wet scrap of paper towel placed in the glass container's bottom will prevent the glue inside of the tip from drying out. Small plastic glue bottles are available at craft supply stores and online.

Decoupage Scissors

Small, sharp, micro-tip scissors are ideal for the fringing and intricate work that's sometimes called for when quilling. But don't use scissors to cut the ends of paper strips—as you measure lengths of strips, tear instead. The glued seams of torn ends are less visible.

Dry-Embossing Tool

In addition to embossing paper strips (see page 25 for instructions on embossing), this tool comes in handy to score paper and make "invisible" marks by pressing down lightly on paper with the rounded metal tip to mark measurements. Embossing tools are available at craft stores and online. You can make your own embossing tool by gluing one metal bead of a different size to each end of a round toothpick. Use an all-purpose or jewelry glue and allow it to dry for a few hours before using the tool.

Metal Pins

Metal 3-inch and larger pins are useful for making spirals (see page 21 for instructions on spiraling). These pins can be purchased online.

Designer Work Board

This is a specialty quilling board made of cork with recessed circle molds made from a plastic template that's attached to the board. The circle molds help you make uniform quilled circles in six sizes. They also store your quilled circles until you're ready to glue or shape them. The large open section is handy for holding straight pins, and the opposite side is bare cork you can cover and use as a work surface. Several types of designer work boards are available online at quilling supply stores. They range from 6 x 8½ inches with 36 molds to 8½ x 11 inches with 106 molds.

Fringing Tool

A fringing tool (available from online quilling stores) is one of the most expensive and sought-after quilling tools. When you thread ¼- to ³⁄₈-inch-wide paper strips through the tool and rapidly move its handle, it quickly makes straight, even cuts along the edge of the paper. This tool is worth the cost if you'll use it frequently and you have volumes of fringed work to do. However, ⅛-inch strips must be hand-fringed, so for these thinner strips you'll

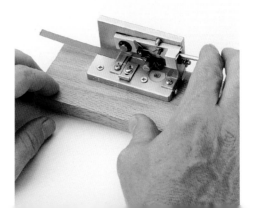

need sharp scissors and a bit more time (see page 23 for instructions on fringing).

Paper Shredder

Many quillers find a paper shredder provides an easy way to make their own strips for quilling. The older type shredder that cuts straight 1/4-inch strips is most popular. Electric and smaller, battery-operated versions can be found at yard sales, office supply stores, and online auctions. (They've become less expensive as confetti-style shredders have become more popular.) One disadvantage is that your paper strips may have rough edges if the blades are dull from wear. Another popular shredder is a small plastic handheld one that cuts 1/8-inch-wide strips by turning a handle. A drawback is that it cuts only up to 3-inch-wide sheets of paper, and the strips are held in a small container. To remedy this, remove the top portion and hold it in one hand while shredding a long strip of 3-inch paper. This shredder is inexpensive, portable, and makes strips with smooth edges. It can be found at big discount stores in the office supply section and online.

Craft Knife

A craft knife is a handy tool to keep nearby to cut materials without dulling your scissors. Use a craft knife with a ruler to cut wide strips of paper. Don't forget a craft knife handle makes a great dowel!

Rotary Cutter

You need a straightedge and a self-healing mat to use a rotary cutter. If you use a bit of pressure when rolling, a rotary cutter will slice through several sheets and thicknesses of paper at one time, making a perfectly even cut. Many quillers who are also quilters use a rotary cutter to make their own paper and use it in place of scissors for straight cutting. Rotary cutters can be found at all fabric and craft stores.

Hand Punches

You'll find a whole variety of hand punches available online and in craft stores. Contemporary quillers often use punches to make punched flowers in different shapes and sizes, and you'll find projects in this book that use the technique of combining punched and quilled flower shapes. Decorative border punches are being used to introduce a new quilling technique. Any small-shape punch can be used with quilling (see Punched Strips, page 25).

BASIC SHAPES AND QUILLING TECHNIQUES

Quilling projects are made of individual shapes. Almost all the shapes start with a circle. The names of the basic shapes are fairly standard: "loose circle," "loose coil," or "loose roll" are terms that all refer to the same shape. The shapes used in this book, and instructions on how to make them, follow.

Circles

Circles (also called "rolls") are one of the most basic shapes in quilling—they're the starting point for many fancier shapes. You can make a circle using either a slotted quilling tool or a needle tool.

Tight Circle Using a Slotted Tool

Thread one end of the paper strip into the tool's slot, making sure that the end of the strip is just at the slot's edge and doesn't stick out past it. Turn the tool as you maintain tension on the paper strip. Remove the circle by gently

slipping the tool from the circle's center. Place a tiny dab of glue on the loose, torn end of the paper strip. Press down to secure, holding it in place for a few seconds until the glue dries.

Use the flat end of your slotted tool to smooth out the top of the tight circle, if necessary. This very simple shape is often used to make flower centers and pegs.

TIP▸ • **If the slotted tool is difficult to remove from the center of the coil or the paper comes out with the tool, you're not threading the paper correctly. Check to be sure that the edge of the strip is inside the slot and not sticking out before starting to roll.**

Tight Circle Using a Needle Tool

Place one end of a paper strip flat against your index finger. Position the needle portion of your needle tool flat against the paper end at a 90-degree angle, and use your thumb to press the paper around the tool. Hold the tool stationary and roll the paper carefully around it to form a tight coil. Be sure to keep the paper edges even. When you're finished, slip the needle tool out from the coil's center, holding the coil together with your fingers. Apply glue and smooth out the top as described above.

Peg

A peg is a tight roll glued behind a quilled shape or section of quilling. The peg raises the piece off the background and gives it height and dimension. To make a peg, follow the instructions for making a tight circle.

Semitight Circle

This shape is used mostly as a larger peg glued under a quilled shape. Make a tight roll and release the tension slightly before gluing the end to increase the size.

Bullet

A bullet shape is made with a short triangular strip of paper. To make one, cut a 1-inch-long strip of paper diagonally from one corner to the other lengthwise. Using your quilling tool (a slotted tool is recommended), roll the paper tightly, beginning at the wide end and keeping the point in the center of the roll. Glue the point to the shape, then remove the completed bullet from the tool. For the projects in this book, you'll use a bullet shape to represent a seed, a coconut, and a flower bud.

Loose Circle

This is the most common quilled shape. It's often pinched and shaped into many other shapes. Begin by rolling a tight circle and leaving it unglued. Lay it on a flat surface and allow the tension to release to create the size of circle needed. Glue the loose end in place.

Teardrop

Pinch one side of a glued loose circle to form a point. Pinch where the loose end was glued so when you glue teardrops together to form a flower, the seams will be hidden.

Shaped Teardrop

Slightly curl the end of a teardrop with your fingers to make a slight curve.

Paisley

Use a small dowel to shape the end of a shaped teardrop into a more prominent curl. Use a toothpick for small shapes and the handle of a slotted tool or 1/8-inch dowel for larger shapes.

Marquise

Pinch opposite sides of a loose circle into points. This is also known as an "eye" shape.

Shaped Marquise

Use your fingers, a toothpick, or a dowel to curl the two pinched points of a marquise in opposite directions. This is also known as a "leaf" shape.

Square

Make a marquise, rotate it 90 degrees, and pinch two more points on the opposite rounded sides.

Diamond

Make a square and push in slightly on two opposite corners.

Crescent

Wrap a loose circle around a dowel while pressing down on the two points that are not exactly opposite one another to form a moon shape. Use your fingers to curl the points toward each other.

Scrolls

Scrolls are shapes with unglued ends. Before beginning, use your fingernail or scissors blade to curl the paper strip slightly in the direction you'll be quilling. This helps the finished piece keep its original shape, especially when altering a scrolled shape into an irregular filigree shape.

S scroll

Roll each end toward the center of the strip to form an S shape.

C scroll

Roll each end toward the center of the strip to form a C shape.

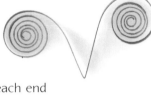

V scroll

Fold the paper strip in half to make a V. Roll each end to the outside almost to the fold.

Open Heart

Fold the paper strip in half to make a V. Roll each end to the inside almost to the fold.

Loose Scroll

Roll a loose circle and leave the end unrolled and unglued.

Tendril

Make a loose scroll and place it on a flat surface. Hold the loose end with one hand and place the point of a straight pin in the center of the coil. Move the pin in the opposite direction from the loose end, gently loosening the roll to make a long, soft curl shape. Tendrils are often used as flowing stems in flower designs.

Folded Roses

To make the center of the rose, begin rolling a paper strip on a slotted quilling tool. Make three complete turns with the tool. Fold the paper away from you, at a right angle. Roll the strip again, keeping its bottom edge right against the tool but allowing its upper edge to flare. Roll until the fold is at the top, make another right-angle fold, and roll again, flaring the paper at the top. Repeat until the rose is the desired size, then glue the end in place.

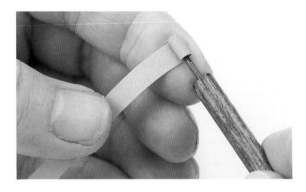

Loops

To begin looping, use one end of a strip to form a loop, then wrap while pinching the end together and making each loop slightly larger or smaller than the preceding one. To begin a five-loop shape, for example, make a $3/8$-inch loop with the end of an 8-inch strip. Bring the paper up beside the first loop and make a second loop slightly taller. Hold the loops in one hand and make the loops with the other. Pinch the bottom of the shape each time you make a loop. The paper is being folded into an accordion as you loop. Make a third loop taller than the second loop. Make the fourth and fifth loop the same size as the second and first loop. Tear paper at the pinched end, wrap around the gathered folds, and glue to the side at the bottom of the shape.

Spirals

Use the needle portion of a needle quilling tool or specialty spiral needle. Place one end of the paper strip at an angle against the tool near the handle, not the tip. Roll the strip, maintaining some tension on the paper with your tool-holding hand, so that the spiral's starting point moves up toward the tip of the tool and off the end. Slightly moisten your fingertips as you make the spiral. Instead of making numerous short spirals, make an extra long spiral and cut the desired lengths with small scissors at an angle to make points on each end. Gluing two spiral ends together makes a connected spiral shape. Apply glue to one end and fit the glued point into the other end. Allow to dry, then shape as desired. A round connected spiral makes a perfect frame for a scrapbook.

Punched Flowers

Use a small flower hand punch to punch out several flowers from a paper strip. Place the flower in the palm of your hand, and while cupping your hand, press in the center with the largest end of an embossing tool until the flower takes shape. If you're making a lot of flowers, you may want to use a small square of craft foam to shape the flowers, so your hand doesn't become sore.

DECORATIVE QUILLING TECHNIQUES

You'll find all sorts of decorative techniques in this book that will add pizzazz to your projects. Texturize your paper strips by crimping or embossing—the choices of motifs for embossing are practically endless! Certain paints specifically formulated for paper are acid-free and provide an easy way to turn plain paper strips into something special—some even make paper look metallic. A touch of chalk on a completed quilled design creates dimension and produces a unique look. Use contrasting chalk colors for depth, or apply black/browns for an antique effect. An

unlimited number of designs can be achieved by punching paper strips, and punched strips can be combined with double quilling. Fringed paper strips are most commonly used for making small flowers and leaves, but the same technique can be used to make tropical palm fronds. And don't forget about adding words and phrases to your projects: shaping paper or metal strips into letters is easier than it looks—very little material is needed for an awesome result.

Crimping

Crimping adds a corrugated texture to paper. You can stack two or three strips of paper on top of one another and roll them through the crimper, or you can roll several strips at the same time side by side. Premeasured strips can be glued together at their ends before crimping, or you can crimp individual strips first and then match up the crimped grooves and glue the ends together. The lengths given for paper in the instructions are the length the paper should be before crimping.

Fringing

Fringing is the process of cutting tiny slits along one edge of a paper strip, using a fringing tool or scissors. To fringe wide strips of paper, use the same process of cutting evenly spaced slits.

Fringed Flowers

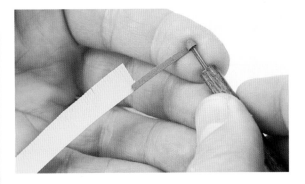

Begin by fringing a paper strip. Use a quilling tool (a slotted tool is recommended) to roll the fringed strip into a tight roll. Glue down the loose end using very little glue and being careful not to get glue on the fringed part of the roll. Use your fingernail or the tip of a straight pin to spread the fringes out into a round flower shape.

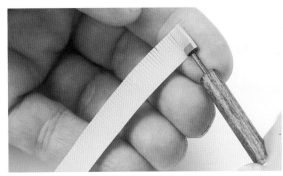

Fringed Flowers with Center

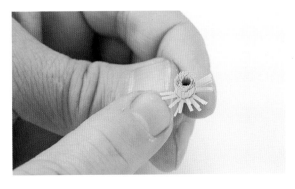

Glue a very narrow strip to the bottom edge of one end of an unrolled fringed strip. Start rolling the narrow strip, keeping the edge straight. The narrow strip will form a center for the fringed flower. When the entire assembly is rolled, glue the end in place and let it dry. Spread out the fringes with your fingernail or the tip of a straight pin.

Double Fringing

A paper strip is fringed, adjusted by either folding or rolling, then fringed again at the same angle to create slivers of paper and a feathery effect.

Double Quilling

Double quilling uses two colors of paper to create visually interesting shapes. In double quilling two strips of contrasting or complementary colors are glued together at one end and then rolled as if one strip. The inner strip (which will be the color inside the quilled shape) should be about $1/4$ inch shorter than the outer strip. Attach the inner strip to the outer strip with a dot of glue about $1/4$ inch down from the end of the outer strip. This leaves the single layer of the outer strip to begin quilling around the tool so getting started is easier. When done rolling, tear off any of the inner strip that extends beyond the end of the outer strip. Glue the end in place.

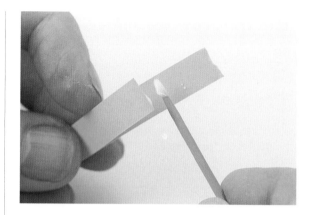

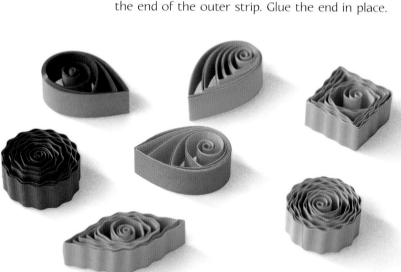

Punched Strips

Use a hand punch to punch shapes in strips of paper before rolling. Paper widths of 3/8 inch and wider work best. A border punch creates lace paper for rolling.

Dry-Embossed Strips

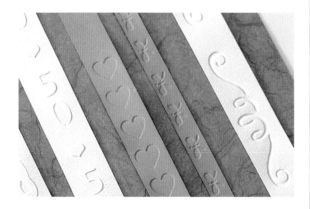

Use the dry-embossing technique on strips of paper before rolling for a unique effect. All you need is an embossing tool and a stencil with a small design. Tape the stencil to the top of a light box or on the glass of a bright window.

Place the paper strip on top of the stencil and outline the design with your tool. Emboss as much of the paper strip as needed. Embossing works best on solid-colored strips and shows up well on vellum strips. Chalk the embossed areas for an added dimensional or an antique effect.

Painted Strips

Have fun with all the paints available for paper! Paint an entire sheet with paper paint, let dry, and then cut your strips to roll. Use foam or rubber stamps with the paint to make a design, let dry, and cut the strips to quill. Use a wide-tip metallic paint pen to paint the back of gold and silver precut and packaged quilling strips.

Chalking

Use colored chalk and a soft chalk applicator to embellish the edges of quilling. Dark brown or black chalk creates an antique effect. Use a darker shade of the same color to create a dimensional effect. Lightly spray your finished work with an acid-free spray fixative or use tissue paper to lightly burnish the chalk to set it.

MAKING LETTERS

Using scrolls and other shapes you can create your own alphabets to add a personal touch to many quilling projects.

Shaping Metal

Strips of metal cut from sheets (purchased at craft stores) can be shaped and glued into letters. Place a letter pattern under your work board cover. Use a toothpick and the handle of a slotted quilling tool to curl the ends. Use larger dowels to shape the curves. The metal bends easily to make folds. If you make a mistake, don't throw away the twisted piece of metal. Flatten it out, and roll over it with your quilling tool handle to smooth it, and then start over. Glue the metal pieces together to form letters and words.

Shaping Paper & Making Letters

Any width of paper strips can be easily shaped and glued into letters. Place a letter pattern under your work board cover. Use your fingernail or scissors blade to barely curl a few strips of paper—this conditions heavier-weight paper to make it easier to work with and shape. Use all sizes of loose scrolls, curved strips, and straight strips to make the shapes. Glue the pieces together to form letters and words.

GLUE-BACKING

Depending on the size of the piece, use a fine-tip glue applicator, a small paintbrush, or your fingertip to cover the acetate's surface with a thin to medium coat of glue in the shape of the piece. Then place the quilled piece on the acetate's surface, right on top of the glue, and let dry completely. When dry, the piece will easily peel off the acetate. Trim off any excess glue around the edges with small scissors. Acrylic paint can be mixed with the glue to make an opaque same-color backing. (This works well with quilled jewelry.) Cardboard backing on a piece can be replaced with an opaque glue-backing.

This is the technique of putting a solid transparent glue covering on the back of a completed quilled shape, so the center will stay in place and the piece will maintain the desired shape. To add a glue-backing, place the quilled piece face-side-up and cover it with a piece of acetate.

EMBOSSED TULIPS

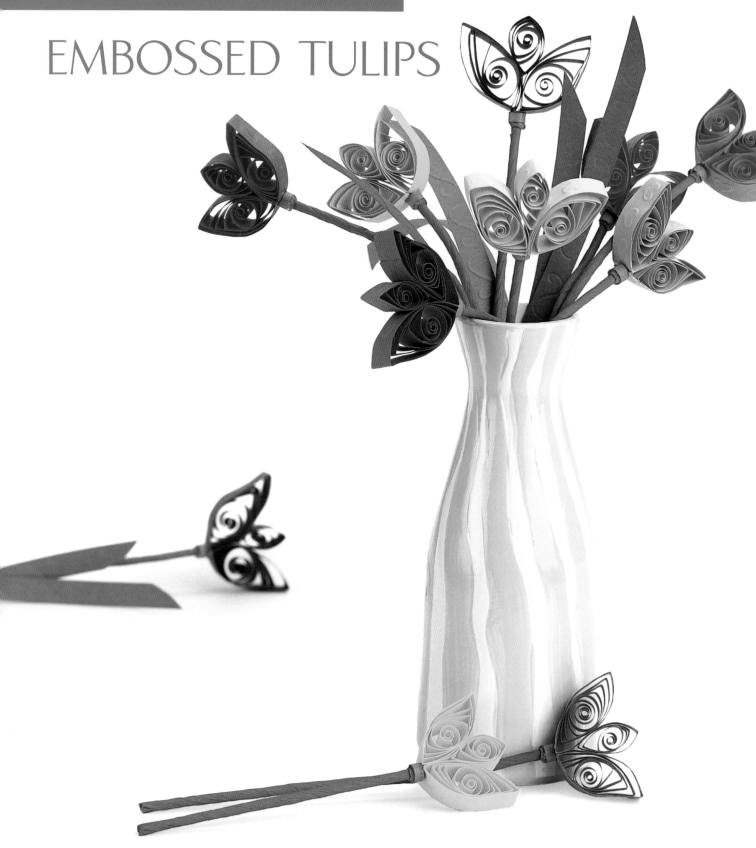

The combination of embossed designs and bright colors on quilled tulip shapes creates a jaunty bouquet. Add just the right vase and you have the perfect little spring accent for any room.

YOU WILL NEED

Basic quilling tool kit (page 8)

3/8-inch-wide paper strips (various bright colors)

Embossing stencils*

Dry-embossing tool

Medium-weight green paper

Covered floral wire

Wire cutters

Sponge brush

Green acrylic paint (same shade as green paper)

Small vase

* Use a motif of your choice for embossing.

BASIC TECHNIQUES USED

Dry embossing (A)
Loose circle (B)
Marquise (C)

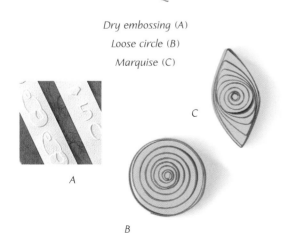

A

B

C

INSTRUCTIONS

1

You'll make 10 tulips altogether. To begin making the first one, tear two $^3/_8$ x 12-inch strips and one $^3/_8$ x 6-inch strip in the color of your choice. Stack the 12-inch strips and emboss them both at the same time. (See page 25 for instructions for dry embossing.) Begin at one end and emboss the motif across the strip until approximately 3 $^1/_2$ inches of the paper are embossed. Leave a $^1/_4$-inch space between each embossed motif. Begin at the edge of the 6-inch strip and emboss the same motif across 2 inches of the strip.

2

Begin rolling at the end opposite from the embossing and make three loose circles: two $^7/_8$ inch in diameter and one $^5/_8$ inch in diameter. Pinch the circles into marquise shapes.

3

Glue approximately $^1/_4$ inch of the ends of the larger shapes together to form the two outer tulip petals (use the tulips in the photo for reference). Glue the small marquise between these petals. Shape the two large petals slightly outward.

4

To make the leaves, first tear a generous amount of green paper in lengths varying from 5 to 8 inches. Trim the tops at an angle. Choose a long flowing design to emboss the leaves—this will save time. Use the blade of your scissors to shape and slightly curve each leaf.

5

Cut 10 pieces of the floral wire in 3 1/2-, 4 1/2-, and 5 1/2-inch lengths. Use the sponge brush to paint the stems with the green paint. Let them dry.

6

To make a stem holder, roll a 1/8 x 4-inch green strip around the end of a painted wire stem. Wrap tightly but loose enough so it can be removed. Remove the stem holder and glue the loose end without losing tension. Make one stem holder for each stem.

7

Using an ample amount of glue, attach a stem holder to the bottom center of each tulip. Allow to dry completely, then glue the stems to the tulips. Lay the flowers on a flat surface and allow to dry for at least 1 hour before handling. Bend the tulip stems as desired. Arrange the flowers and leaves in the vase.

TIP▶• When shaping a marquise, always pinch where the loose end is glued to keep the seam hidden at the point. In this project, glue all the petals with the seams down and inside for a flawless flower.

SPECIAL OCCASION CARDS

These delightful cards are perfect for any occasion— and oh-so-easy to create. Your friends and loved ones may never be satisfied with store-bought cards again!

YOU WILL NEED

Basic quilling tool kit (page 8)
1/8-inch-wide paper strips (various colors)
Pearl beads (optional)
Decorative paper scraps
Blank greeting card, any size

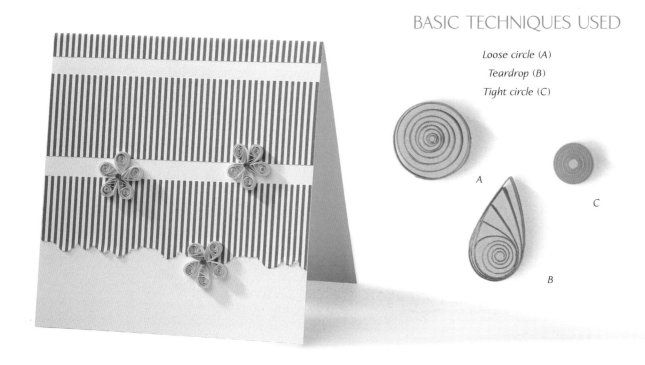

BASIC TECHNIQUES USED

Loose circle (A)

Teardrop (B)

Tight circle (C)

INSTRUCTIONS

1

To begin making a five-petal flower (you'll make three of these), tear five 5-inch-long strips. Roll five loose circles, making sure all the circles are the same size.

2

Pinch the loose circles into teardrop shapes. Glue the teardrops together at the points to form a flower.

3

Glue a pearl to center of flower, and set it aside to dry. (Alternatively, you can cut a $1/8$ x 2-inch paper strip of any color in half lengthwise, roll it into a tight circle, and use it for a flower center.) Make two more flowers.

4

Cut or tear decorative paper into various shapes and glue them to the front of the card as desired (see photos for ideas). Arrange flowers on the card and glue them in place. Let dry.

TIP▸● If you're mailing the card, protect the quilled shapes with layers of tissue paper or bubble wrap before placing the card in an envelope. Slip the envelope into a thin mailing box or a padded envelope for additional protection.

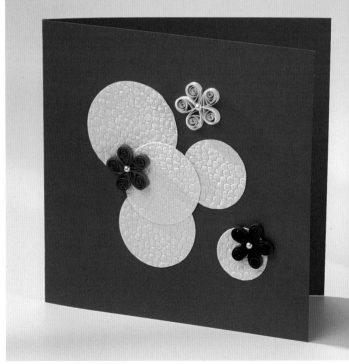

SUMMER CANDLE RING

Dress up a plain candle for a bright summer centerpiece.
A colorful bandanna, rolled up tightly and tied in the back,
can be used in lieu of the fabric-covered floral ring
for an even quicker project.

YOU WILL NEED

Basic quilling tool kit (page 8)
$1/_4$-inch-wide paper strips (red, green,
lime green, and black)
Paper crimper
$1/_2$- and $3/_4$-inch dowels (or similar-size
cylindrical object)
Opaque white paint pen or white paint
4-inch foam floral ring
$1/_3$ yards fabric ribbon,
approximately $1/_2$ inches wide
Fabric glue
Straight pins
Heat-resistant decorative plate
Pillar candle

BASIC TECHNIQUES USED

Loose circle (A)
Crescent (B)
Teardrop (C)
Tight bullet (D

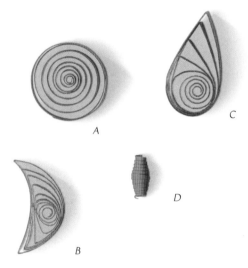

A

C

D

B

INSTRUCTIONS

1

Glue ¼-inch red strips end-to-end to make eight 24-inch, six 36-inch, and three 48-inch strips. Run all these red strips through the paper crimper. Crimp six ¼ x 12-inch green strips and four 10-inch lime green strips for rinds and set aside.

2

To make a round slice, first roll a loose circle approximately 1¼ inches in diameter using a 48-inch red strip. Glue the end of a lime green strip to the outside of the loose circle and wrap

it around twice. Tear the strip and glue the end. Repeat, using the green paper, but wrap this strip around three times before gluing the end. Make two more round slices.

3

To make a large crescent-shaped slice, roll a loose circle approximately 1¼ inches in diameter using a 36-inch red strip. The tension will be very loose so that it can be shaped into a crescent. Wrap the circle around the ¾-inch dowel, pressing down on both ends to make points. Use your fingers to finish shaping, pressing in the center if necessary.

4

Wrap two layers of lime green to the outside curve of the crescent, and then wrap three layers of green over the lime green. Make five more large crescent-shaped slices.

5

To make a small crescent-shaped slice, roll a loose circle approximately 1 inch in diameter using a 24-inch red strip. The tension will once again be very loose. Wrap the circle around the ½-inch dowel, pressing down on the two ends to make points. Use your fingers to finish shaping, pressing in the center if necessary. Wrap two layers of lime green to the outside curve of the crescent, then wrap three layers of the green over the lime green. Make five more small crescent-shaped slices.

6

To make a wedge-shaped slice (see the slice on the upper left side of the ring in the photo for reference), roll one of two remaining 24-inch strips into a 1-inch-diameter loose circle. Pinch one end to make a teardrop. Go up about 3/4 inch from the teardrop point, and pinch to make another point. Repeat on the other side of the teardrop point, coming up about 3/4 inch, pinching, and making a third point. This should give you a shape that looks like a pie slice. Apply two layers of lime green and three layers of green as described above to make the rind.

7

Apply a glue-backing (see page 27) to all watermelon pieces, and allow to dry completely before adding seeds.

8

To make the seeds, you'll need a strip of paper that's just a bit narrower than 1/4 inch. Trim about a 1/16-inch strip off the top of a black 1/4-inch-wide strip. Tear this narrower strip into 1 1/4-inch lengths. Cut each of these diagonally in half lengthwise, from one corner to the opposite corner, making long triangles. Begin rolling tightly at the wide end of the strip (a slotted quilling tool is suggested). Glue the roll at the pointed end. Glue three seeds to the smaller quilled pieces and five or more to the large round watermelon shapes. Let the seeds dry, then use a paint pen or paint and a toothpick to highlight the seeds with dots of white.

9

To make the candle ring, place the floral ring on a flat surface. Wrap 1 yard of fabric ribbon around the ring. Secure the end at the bottom of the ring with fabric glue and straight pins. Make a bow with the remaining 12-inch length of ribbon. Attach the bow to the front top of the ring with fabric glue and straight pins and let dry.

10

Place quilled pieces around the candle ring, then glue to the top and sides with fabric glue. Place the assembly on the plate and add a pillar candle. And don't forget: Never leave a burning candle unattended!

BEAUTIFUL BOWS

Look what you can create using three (count 'em) simple styles of bows.
Make them large, small, or in-between. Crimp the paper or leave it smooth.
Use solid or patterned paper. The variations are endless.

YOU WILL NEED

Basic quilling tool kit (page 8)

Paper trimmer

Paper crimper

Card stock in bright colors

Removable double-stick tape

Paper punch, 1/2-inch flower

Hand punch, 1/4-inch flower

Gift boxes

Permanent double-stick tape (optional)

BASIC TECHNIQUES USED

Loose circle (A)

Teardrop (B)

Note: In the front row of the photo are from left to right examples of formal bows, a flower bow, and a bridge bow.

INSTRUCTIONS
LARGE FORMAL BOW

1

Cut and crimp three $1^3/8$ x 11-inch strips of card stock. Roll two of these into $1^1/2$-inch-diameter loose circles. Pull the center of each circle toward the glued seam with tweezers, then pinch to shape into teardrops.

2

Glue the two points together and allow to dry. Cut the remaining strip into a 4-inch strip and a 7-inch strip. Roll the 4-inch strip into a $1/2$-inch-diameter loose circle. Glue this onto the center of the bow as shown in the photo.

3

Use the remaining 7-inch strip for the bow tail. Cut the ends of the tail at an angle (or fishtail) and curl slightly with scissors blades. Glue the bow on top of the tail. Let dry, then use removable double-stick tape to adhere the bow to a gift box.

SMALL FORMAL BOW

1

Cut and crimp three $5/8$ x 11-inch strips of card stock. Roll two of these into 1-inch-diameter loose circles. Pull the center of each circle toward the glued seam with tweezers, then pinch to shape into teardrops.

2

Glue the two points together and allow to dry. Cut 4 inches from the remaining strip and roll this into a loose circle ¼ inch in diameter. Glue this onto the center of the bow as shown in the photo.

3

Use 5 inches of the remaining strip for the bow tail. Cut the ends of the tail at an angle and curl slightly with scissors blades. Glue the bow on top of the bow tail. Let dry, then adhere the bow to a gift box with removable double-stick tape.

LARGE FLOWER BOW

NOTE▶ • While these instructions call for five petals, you can also make flower bows with six petals if you choose.

1

Cut and crimp five ¾ x 11-inch strips of card stock. Make five loose circles 1¼ inches in diameter.

2

Pull the center of each loose circle toward the glued seam with the tweezers, then pinch to shape into teardrops. Glue the points of the five teardrops together to make a flower.

3

Punch a ½-inch flower shape. Glue the flower shape to the center of the flower created in the previous step. Cut and crimp a 1 x 11-inch strip for the bow tail. Trim the ends to the desired lengths, then curl the ends slightly with scissors blades. Glue the flower bow on top of the tail. Let dry, then use removable double-stick tape to adhere the bow to a gift box.

TIP▶ • While you should use all-purpose glue for gluing shapes—depending on the type of

paper and size of the bow—you may find it easier (and faster) to use permanent double-stick tape to adhere the bow to the bow tail. Experiment and decide for yourself.

SMALL FLOWER BOW

1

Cut and crimp five ⅜ x 8-inch strips of card stock. Make five loose circles ¾ inch in diameter.

2

Pull the center of each loose circle toward the glued seam with the tweezers, then pinch to shape into teardrops. Glue the points of the five teardrops together to make a flower.

3

Punch a ¼-inch flower shape. Glue the flower shape to the center of the flower created in the previous step. Cut and crimp a ½ x 8-inch strip for the bow tail. Trim the ends to the desired lengths, then curl the ends slightly with scissors blades. Glue the flower bow on top of the tail. Let dry, then use removable double-stick tape to adhere the bow to a gift box.

LARGE BRIDGE BOW

1

Cut and crimp five 1 x 8½-inch strips of card stock. Roll these into five 1-inch-diameter loose circles. Pull the center of each circle toward the glued seam with the tweezers, then pinch to shape into teardrops.

2

Glue two shapes point to point and allow to dry. Glue the remaining three pieces on top as shown in the photo.

3

Cut and crimp a 1¼ x 8½-inch strip for the bow tail. Cut the ends of the tail at an angle or fold the ends first and then cut them at an angle to fishtail them. Curl the ends slightly with scissors blades. Glue the bow on top of the tail. Let dry, then use removable double-stick tape to adhere the bow to a gift box.

SMALL BRIDGE BOW

1

Cut and crimp five ⅜ x 6-inch strips of card stock. Roll these into five ½-inch-diameter loose circles. Pull the center of each circle toward the glued seam with the tweezers, then pinch to shape into teardrops.

2

Glue two shapes point to point and allow them to dry. Glue the remaining three pieces on top as shown in the photo.

3

Cut and crimp a ½ x 8-inch strip for the bow tail. Cut the ends of the tail at an angle or fold the ends first and then cut them at an angle to fishtail them. Curl the ends slightly with scissors blades. Glue the bow on top of the tail. Let dry, and then use removable double-stick tape to adhere the bow to a gift box.

TIP ➤ • Premade quilled bows are a tremendous time-saver. Keep the bows and tails separate. If you have a premade six-petal flower bow and it's the wrong size or shape for a particular gift box, remove one of the petals and it becomes a bridge bow. If the flower bow has five petals, gently separate two petals.

BUTTONED UP GIFT BAGS

No doubt about it. anyone who receives these gift bags will be reluctant to unbutton them. Make these toppers ahead of time and keep them handy to dress up those spur of the moment gifts. They're cute as a you-know-what.

YOU WILL NEED

Basic quilling tool kit (page 8)

1/4-inch-wide paper strips

(in three coordinating colors)

Paper crimper

Card stock (same colors as paper strips)

Paper punch, 3/4-inch circle

Hand punch, 1/16- and 1/8-inch circles

Decorative-edge scissors

Paper gift bag

Vellum, white or translucent

3/4-inch ribbon, matching or coordinating color

BASIC TECHNIQUE USED

Loose circle

INSTRUCTIONS

1

Tear two 12-inch strips of one color for the inside of the button and one 12-inch strip of another color for the outside of the button. Glue the strips end-to-end and run this through the paper crimper.

2

Begin rolling at the inside-color end of the strip. Make a loose circle approximately 1 inch in diameter, then glue the loose end to the side. Punch a 3/4-inch circle from card stock, the same color as the inside color of the button, and glue it to the back.

3

Use either the third coordinating color or the outside button color to make the buttonholes. Punch out four circles from paper strips (or card stock) with the 1/16-inch hand punch, then glue them to the button, using the photo for reference. Alternate colors, and repeat steps 1 through 3 to make the second and third buttons.

4

Cut a piece of card stock to 5 inches in length. Measure the width of the bag you'll be decorating, and subtract 1/2 inch. Cut the card stock's width to this measurement. Fold the rectangle of card stock in half lengthwise. Use decorative-edge scissors to cut around the edges.

5

Unfold the card stock and place it right-side-up on a flat surface. Lay a piece of same-size vellum on top. Cut or tear the vellum (use a ruler for tearing) into a rectangle that's slightly smaller than the piece of card stock.

6

Fold both pieces in half and place them over the top of the gift bag. Use the 1/8-inch circle hand punch to punch two holes 1/2 inch apart at the top for the ribbon, but don't add the ribbon yet.

7

Center the three buttons on the vellum and glue them in place. Allow them to completely dry.

8

Cut a 6-inch length of ribbon and trim the ends diagonally. Thread both ends (separately) into the holes at the front of the bag. Turn the bag around and crisscross the ribbon ends, then rethread them back into the opposite holes from the ones they came through. (Use tweezers to help guide the ends back through a second time.) Pull the ribbon ends gently in the front to tighten, and trim the ends evenly at angles or fold each end in half and trim at an angle to create a fishtail.

CANDY TOPPERS

These irresistible decorations will be the talk of every holiday gathering! Easy to make and fun to give, these quilled toppers will inspire you to create your own for other holiday celebrations.

YOU WILL NEED

Basic quilling tool kit (page 8)

¹/8-inch-wide paper strips (various colors, see instructions)

Designer work board (optional)

Small hand punches (various shapes)

Decorative-edge scissors

¹/8-inch dowel

Pen (or similar-sized object)

Decorative papers

Miniature chocolate candy bars

Tape

White craft matchboxes

BASIC TECHNIQUES USED

Loose circle (A)
Teardrop (B)
Tight circle (C)
Marquise (D)
Semitight circle (E)
V scroll (F)

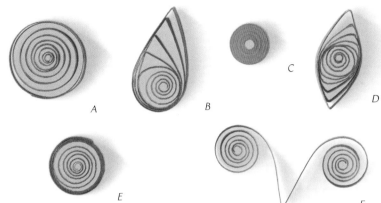

INSTRUCTIONS

WITCH'S HAT

1

Use a ⅛ x 16-inch strip of black paper for the pointed part of the hat. Make a loose circle approximately ¾ inch in diameter. Pinch one side to shape the circle into a teardrop, then press the opposite end down on a flat surface to make a flat edge approximately ½ inch across.

2

Wrap the flat edge around the dowel to curve slightly. Bend the top portion of the pointed end slightly to one side.

3

Use a ⅛ x 12-inch strip of bright green, orange, or purple paper for the brim. Roll a loose circle approximately ⅝ inch in diameter and shape it into a marquise. Wrap it around the pen barrel to shape into a curve.

4

Glue the hat top to the brim and let dry.

SNOWFLAKES

1

Use white, gray, and light blue ⅛-inch-wide paper strips to make the snowflakes. For each snowflake, tear 13 strips of paper to 1½ inches in length.

2

Roll one semitight circle, glue the loose end, and place it on a clear sheet of

acetate. Make six marquise shapes and six V scrolls from the remaining strips.

3

Use the photo for reference when assembling the snowflakes. Glue the six marquise shapes evenly around the semitight circle.

4

Glue the inside of the pointed end of each V scroll together. Then glue the curled end of the V scrolls to the marquise shapes as shown.

ASSEMBLY

1

Cut a 1-3/8 x 3-inch piece of decorative paper and use it to cover a piece of miniature candy, taping the ends on the bottom. Use only a dot of glue to adhere the quilled piece on top. Let dry, then group the candies together in a container.

2

Alternatively, you can cut (or tear using the edge of a ruler) a 1 3/4 x 4 1/2-inch piece of decorative paper, and wrap the paper around a white matchbox cover, taping the ends on the bottom. Use only a dot of glue to adhere the quilled piece on top. Fill the matchbox with tiny surprises such as candy, money, small trinkets, or a handwritten note.

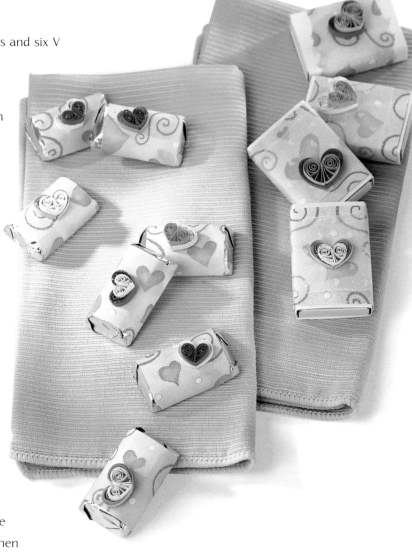

STACKED HEARTS

1

Use 1/8-inch-wide red, pink, and white strips to make the stacked hearts. Tear 4-, 6-, and 8-inch strips of each color. Use two strips of the same color and length to roll two matching loose circles.

2

Shape each into a teardrop by pinching one end. Glue the teardrops together at the sides to make a heart.

3

Make an even number of hearts of various colors and sizes. To make the double hearts, glue a smaller heart onto a larger heart of a different color.

DECORATED EGGS

1

Use a ⅛ x 24-inch strip of paper for each egg. Roll a tight circle and allow it to release into a ¾-inch circle. This is easiest if you have a designer work board and allow the tight circle to release in a ¾-inch circle mold.

2

Pull the center to one side of the circle with tweezers. If using a circle mold, remove the circle from the mold while maintaining your hold with the tweezers. Glue down the loose end of the strip with a dot of glue and apply glue to the area that the tweezers are holding in place.

3

Place the glued side down on a sheet of acetate and press firmly for a few seconds to make sure it doesn't uncoil. When it's completely dry, remove the circle from the acetate. Gently press in the sides to make an egg shape.

4

Decorate the top (unglued) side of the eggs with various colors and shapes of paper. Use hand punches and decorative scissors to create a variety of shapes. After the egg is dec-orated, use small scissors to trim any excess paper at the edges of each piece.

TIP▶ • While not absolutely necessary, it is helpful to apply a glue-backing to each piece because it will keep the shapes intact until assembly. It will also allow the quilled piece to be easily removed from the wrapper and reused for cards, scrapbook pages, or gift tags! (See page 27 for instructions for the glue-backing technique.)

LADYBUG GARDEN HAT

Ever wonder why something is as cute as a bug?
Here's your answer. Hang this charming straw
hat on a chair for an eye-catching spring and
summer decorative accessory.

YOU WILL NEED

Basic quilling tool kit (page 8)
¹/8-inch-wide paper strips (bright red,
orange, yellow-gold, and black)
¹/8-inch dowel
Hand punch, ¹/8-inch circle
Large leaf punch or die-cut leaf
Medium-weight green paper
2 yards of gingham ribbon, 1 inch wide
Small straw hat
Hot glue gun and glue sticks (optional)
Craft wire
Wire cutters

BASIC TECHNIQUES USED

Loose circle (A)

Marquise (B)

Teardrop (C)

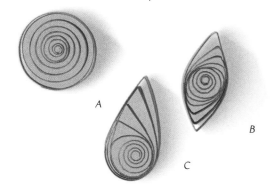

A

B

C

INSTRUCTIONS

1

For each ladybug, roll two 16-inch-long strips of red, orange, or yellow-gold paper into loose circles, then pinch the circles into marquise shapes.

2

Using the photo for reference, place the marquise shapes side by side and glue a portion of the inside edges together to form the ladybug's body.

3

Roll a loose circle from a 4-inch-long black strip. Pinch one side to shape the circle into a teardrop, then press the opposite end down on a flat surface to make a flat edge approximately 3/8 inch across. Curve the ends of the flat edge toward the point to make an odd-shaped triangle. This piece will fit into the bottom of the body, in the space where the marquise pieces aren't glued together. Glue in place and hold for a few seconds while it dries to ensure a rounded shape.

4

Roll a loose circle from a 2 1/2-inch-long black strip. Press the side against the dowel to make a moon shape. Glue on top of the body for the head. Punch out five or six black dots with the circle punch and glue these dots randomly to the body.

5

Follow the instructions on page 27 to add a glue-backing to all the quilled ladybug pieces. Allow to dry completely.

6

Use the large leaf punch or die-cut to create leaves. Make enough leaves to cover most of the hat brim.

7

Cut the ribbon into two 1-yard pieces. Wrap 1 yard around the bottom of the hat's crown, tying in a knot at the back. Hot-glue the ribbon to the hat if necessary. Tie the remaining yard of ribbon into a bow, as shown in the photo. Hide the knot in the band by securing the bow to the hat with a short length of wire. Trim the ends of the ribbons at an angle or fold each end in half and cut it at an angle to fishtail the ends.

8

Arrange the leaves and quilled ladybugs around the brim of the hat, using the photo as a guide. Glue all the pieces to the hat. Allow to dry for a few hours.

TIP▶• Now that you have the knack for making adorable quilled ladybugs, use them on cards, scrapbook pages, or accessory boxes!

SUNNY SUNFLOWER WREATH

Wreaths are a wonderful way to decorate your home or office year round. The bright summery colors of sunflowers paired with winsome little bees will make you smile any time of the year.

YOU WILL NEED

Basic quilling tool kit (page 8)

3/8-inch-wide paper strips

(yellow-gold, black, and brown)

Paper crimper

Black card stock

Red chalk

Spray fixative

Photocopier or tracing paper

Leaf patterns (page 122)

Green medium-weight paper

10-inch foam floral ring

Craft knife or sandpaper

Raffia

Hot glue and hot-glue gun

Large, multiloop ribbon bow

1/4-inch-wide paper strips (bright yellow,

black, and light yellow)

BASIC TECHNIQUES USED

Chalking (page 25)

Loose circle (A)

Marquise (B)

Semitight roll (C)

Teardrop (D)

V scroll (E)

Note: Crimp all paper after measuring, except where noted.

A

B

C

D

E

INSTRUCTIONS

1

To make the petals for one sunflower, roll sixteen 3/8 x 8-inch yellow-gold strips into 1-inch-diameter loose circles, then pinch each into a marquise shape.

2

To begin making the center for one sunflower, glue two 3/8 x 12-inch black strips end-to-end to create a 24-inch strip. Glue six 3/8 x 12-inch brown strips end-to-end to create a 72-inch strip. Glue one end of the long brown strip to one end of the long black strip.

3

Starting at the black end of the joined strips, roll tight twice around the quilling tool. Remove the paper from the tool and continue rolling a semitight circle with your fingers. Place the finished circle on a flat surface and let the tension release to 1 3/4-inches in diameter. Glue down the loose end.

4

Holding the flower center in both hands, push up with your thumbs at the bottom of the circle to make a slight dome shape. Cut a 2-inch-diameter circle from the black card stock. Apply glue underneath all around the inside and the bottom edge of the dome shape, then glue it to the center of the black circle. A $1/4$-inch lip of card stock should show around the sunflower's center. Handle this piece on the sides until completely dry.

5

Imagine the quilled dome-shaped center as a clock, and glue a petal to the center at the 12, 3, 6, and 9 o'clock positions. Glue three petals between each of these four petals, being sure to apply an ample amount of glue at the pointed ends, under the points, and to the sides. This will ensure that the petals adhere to the sunflower center, the lip of the card stock circle, and each other. Make two more sunflowers and allow each to dry completely.

6

Apply the red chalk to the glued interior points of the petals, being sure to use a chalk applicator that's small enough to reach inside and around the points. Hold the sunflower upside down (outdoors) to let any loose chalk fall off, then spray the chalked area lightly with a spray fixative.

7

Photocopy or trace the three leaf patterns on page 122. Use these to cut leaves from the green paper. (You can stack sheets of paper to cut several leaves at a time.) Fold the leaves in half lengthwise and run them through the paper crimper at an angle. Unfold. The number of leaves needed will vary—cover as much or as little of the wreath front as desired.

8

Use the craft knife to round the edges of the floral ring. (You can also use coarse sandpaper or your fingers to press and form the wreath.) Gather about 20 strands of raffia together and tie one end of the bunch at the back of the wreath with a single strand of raffia. Start wrapping the thick strand of raffia around the wreath at an angle. When you get to the end of the raffia strand, tie on another thick bunch of raffia and continue wrapping until the entire wreath is covered. Trim any long strands used for tying.

9

To make the bumblebee, double-quill $1/4$ x 7-inch strips of bright yellow and black paper. The outer color should be yellow. (See page 000 for instructions for the double-quilling technique.) Roll a semitight circle $3/4$ inch in diameter, and then shape it into a teardrop. Roll two $1/2$-inch-diameter loose circles from two $1/4$ x 7-inch strips of light yellow paper. Shape these into teardrops for the wings. Tear two $1/4$ x $1 1/2$-inch strips of black paper. Do not crimp these pieces. Make a loose circle for the head and a V scroll for the antenna. Arrange the pieces as shown in the photo and glue. Let dry.

10

Using the photo as a guide to placement, hot-glue the leaves, sunflowers, bumblebee, and the bow to the wreath.

DRAGONFLY PLANT POKES

This trio of colorful, quilled dragonflies gives any potted plant a bit of pizzazz. They're so easy to make and versatile. Use this dragonfly motif to add a touch of nature and dimension to any craft project.

YOU WILL NEED

Basic quilling tool kit (page 8)

$1/4$-inch-wide paper strips (dark, medium, and light pink; black, white)

Paper crimper

Black or metallic craft wire, 24 gauge

$1/8$-inch dowel

Hand punch, $1/4$-inch circle

Rhinestones

Wooden stake

BASIC TECHNIQUES USED

Looping (see illustration)

Bullet (A)

Loose circle (B)

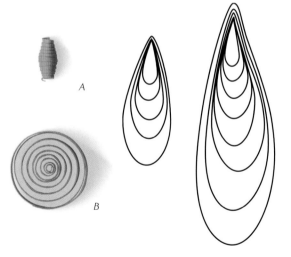

INSTRUCTIONS

1

Use dark, medium, and light pink paper strips to make the top wings. Tear a 6-inch strip from the dark pink paper, an 8-inch strip from the medium pink paper, and a 12-inch strip from the light pink paper. Glue these strips together end-to-end in that order, overlapping the ends slightly. Allow the glue to dry, and then crimp the entire strip.

2

Make a $1/4$-inch fold at the dark end of the strip to begin looping. Make eight loops, allowing a bit more space between each loop and the next as the loops get larger. Glue the end of the strip at the bottom of the loop and tear off any excess. Use this same method to make the second wing, comparing it to the first as you work to make sure they'll end up the same size.

3

To make the bottom wings, first tear a 4-inch strip from the medium pink paper and a 6-inch strip from the light pink paper, then glue the strips together, overlapping the ends slightly. Allow the glue to dry, then crimp the entire strip. Begin looping following the same method used for the top wings, but make five loops for these smaller bottom wings. Make two matching bottom wings, then set all four looped wings aside.

4

Tear a 4-inch strip of black paper for the base of the body. Round one end with scissors for the head. Crimp four black and four white 4-inch paper strips. Make these into eight loose circles that are approximately 3/8 inch in diameter. Apply glue to the side (at the seam) of a black loose circle and glue it to the body's base about 1/4 inch down from the rounded end. Alternate gluing the remaining seven white and black loose circles onto the body's base. Trim any of the base strip that extends beyond the last glued circle.

5

Cut a 1/4 x 1 1/2-inch strip of black paper in half lengthwise. Cut one 1/8 x 1 1/2-inch strip diagonally to get two long triangles. Roll the two triangles into bullet shapes. Bend a 2-inch-long piece of the wire in the center to make a V shape for the antenna. Loosely curl each end of the wire around the dowel several times. Glue a bullet shape to each end of the antenna.

6

Use an ample amount of glue to attach the wire antenna to the top of the body at the rounded end. Punch a 1/4-inch dot from a black strip of paper and place it over the glued-down wire for the head.

7

Roll two bullet shapes using a 2 x 1/4-inch piece of black paper cut into two triangles. Glue these on top of the head for the eyes. Glue small rhinestones on top of the bullet-shaped eyes.

8

Glue the wings to the top portion of the body as shown in the photo. Allow to dry completely. If needed, reshape the wire antennas. Attach the quilled dragonfly to a wooden stake and insert it in an indoor plant.

SWEET RECIPE MEMORIES ALBUM

Life can be a bowl of cherries! Preserve memories of sweet and savory recipes with a retro look— rickrack and stylish cherry motifs. If your tastebuds long for other fruits, choose one of the Carmen Miranda Magnets on page 88.

YOU WILL NEED

Basic quilling tool kit (page 8)

1/8-inch-wide paper strips

(red, bright green, and green)

1/8-inch dowel

Kitchen theme and plaid decorative papers

Spiral journal, 6 x 6 inches

Letter stickers

BASIC TECHNIQUES USED

Loose circle (A)

Shaped marquise (B)

Spiral (C)

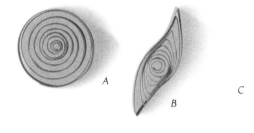

INSTRUCTIONS

1

To make a cherry, roll a 1/8 x 12-inch strip of red paper into a loose circle. Press a 1/8-inch dowel against the side to make a slight indention for the top. Repeat to make two more cherries.

2

To make the leaves, roll four loose circles using four 1/8 x 10-inch strips of bright green paper. Pinch these four loose circles into shaped marquises.

3

The stems are made from spirals (see page 21). Make three spirals with 3-inch green strips. Trim two of these spirals at 1 1/4 inches and the third at 1 3/4 inches.

4

For the rickrack trim, roll 1/8 x 4-inch red strips into loose circles and pinch into shaped marquises. Make as many as needed to fit across two edges of the journal cover.

5

Glue the decorative paper to the book cover. Cut a 1 x 6-inch strip and a 1/2 x 6-inch strip from decorative plaid paper. Adhere these to the bottom and right side of the journal's front cover. Use letter stickers to add a title of your choice across the top.

6

Arrange and glue the cherry pieces, using the photo for reference. Glue the shaped marquise pieces end-to-end (slightly overlapping) across the bottom and right side of the book cover—to create the rickrack design, make sure all the pieces are facing the same direction.

TIP▶• Add a dated message inside the front cover if you're giving this as a gift. Very often family recipe books are handed down through generations. Adhere square envelopes to the first few pages to hold recipe cards.

GRACEFUL SCRIPT ALPHABET

Quilling is perfect for making graceful, curved shapes for an alphabet. Use the script to create elegant embellishments for almost any project you can imagine.

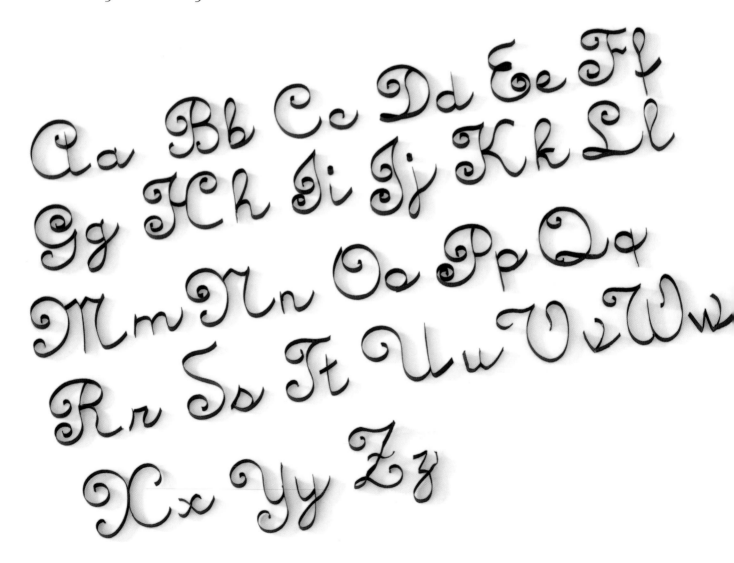

YOU WILL NEED

Basic quilling tool kit (page 8)

Photocopier or tracing paper

*Strips of paper or metal**

¹/8-inch dowel

Jewelry glue (optional)

* Width of strips will depend on size of letters you make.

BASIC TECHNIQUE USED

Shaping

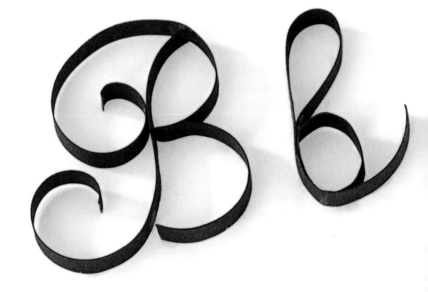

INSTRUCTIONS

1

Photocopy the script alphabet template on page 121, reducing or enlarging as needed for your project. Alternatively, trace the letters needed. Place the alphabet pattern or traced letters under a piece of clear acetate.

2

Cut paper or metal to the width desired; in general, use smaller widths for smaller letters and larger widths for bigger letters. Estimate the length of paper or metal needed for a letter and tear off or cut to size.

3

Shape curves with the handle of the slotted tool or a ¹/8-inch dowel. Make tight curves by shaping around a toothpick or similar-size tool. Many letters will consist of several pieces and shapes.

4

After all pieces are shaped and made, begin gluing shapes together to make completed letters. (Allow to dry at least one hour if using metal.) Then glue the letters together to make words or phrases. (If using metal, allow words to dry overnight, and use jewelry glue to adhere words to your surface.)

ALTERED BOOK NICHE & TAG

Expand your quilling vocabulary with words and phrases created with thin strips of metal. You'll be surprised how easily metal can be shaped to add one-of-a-kind effects to altered book niches, creative tags, or any other project your heart desires.

YOU WILL NEED

Basic quilling tool kit (page 8)

Photocopier or tracing paper

Paper trimmer

Metallic sheet metal*

Jewelry glue

1/8-inch dowel

* *Craft sheet metal is made in metallic shades and colors.*

BASIC TECHNIQUE USED

Shaping

INSTRUCTIONS

1

Photocopy the script alphabet on page 121, reducing or enlarging as needed for your project. Alternatively, trace the letters needed. Place the alphabet pattern or traced letters under a sheet of clear acetate.

2

Use the paper trimmer to cut two strips of the sheet metal. (For our project, we used a 1/4 x 12-inch metal strip to make the letters in the word "create," and a 1/8 x 6-inch strip for the word "art.") Review the script alphabet instructions on page 59. Estimate the length of a piece of sheet metal needed for a letter and cut to size.

3

Shape curves with a 1/8-inch dowel. Make tight curves by shaping around a toothpick or a similar-size tool. Many letters will consist of several pieces and shapes of metal. (If you make a mistake when shaping for a letter, don't throw away the piece of metal: Flatten it and roll over it with your quilling tool handle to smooth it, then start over.)

4

After you've made all the shapes needed, begin gluing the shapes together to make completed letters. Allow the shapes to dry completely before gluing the letters together to create a word.

5

Allow the word to dry overnight. Use jewelry glue to adhere the word to your art piece.

TIP▶• Trimming metal narrower than 1/4 inch wide is difficult. Make a 1/8-inch-wide strip by cutting a 1/4-inch-wide strip in half lengthwise with scissors.

FILLIPED ALPHABET

A little fillip is all that's needed to make an alphabet stand out from the crowd. Shape your letters and you'll be pleasantly surprised at the difference a curl makes.

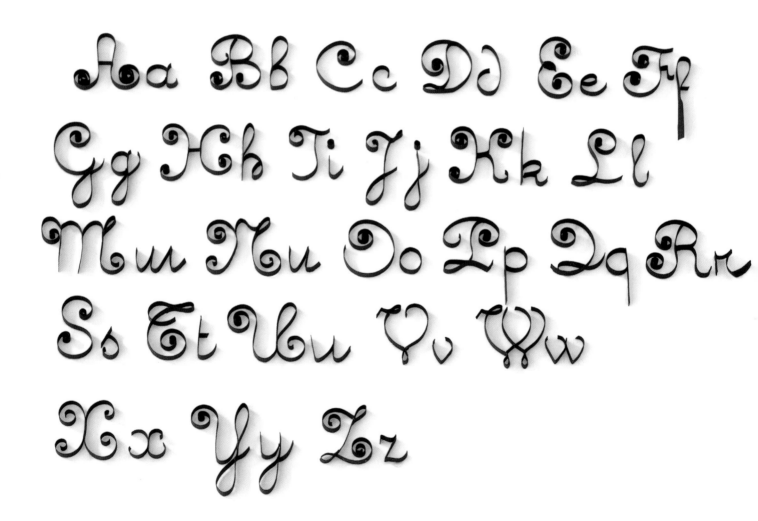

YOU WILL NEED

Basic quilling tool kit (page 8)

Photocopier or tracing paper

*Strips of paper**

1/8-inch dowel

* *Width of strips will depend on size of letters you make.*

BASIC TECHNIQUES USED

Loose scroll

Shaping

INSTRUCTIONS

1

Photocopy the curled-end alphabet on page 120, reducing or enlarging as needed for your project. Alternatively, trace the letters needed for your project. Place the alphabet pattern or traced letters under a piece of clear acetate.

2

Choose the width strips desired for your project; in general, use smaller widths for smaller letters and larger widths for bigger letters. Estimate the length of a strip needed for a letter (or part of a letter) and tear to size.

3

Make a very loose scroll by rolling the paper tightly three or four times around a quilling tool. Unroll and reroll loosely with your fingers. Use this same technique for the curled ends of a letter. Shape curves with the handle of the slotted tool or a 1/8-inch dowel. Make tight curves by shaping around a toothpick or a similar-size tool.

4

After all the pieces needed are quilled and shaped, begin gluing them together to make completed letters. Allow the individual letters to dry before using them in a project.

FRAMED MONOGRAM

Bold copper monograms in a weathered, rustic frame
are a perfect quilled gift for any man in your life.
Use the same alphabet in paler colors, set into a delicate
frame to personalize a gift for her.

YOU WILL NEED

Basic quilling tool kit (page 8)

Photocopier or tracing paper

3/4 x 11-inch painted strips of heavy paper*

Metallic paint, copper

Sponge brush

1/8-inch dowel

Decorative background paper

Shadow box or frame

* This monogram was made with two 3/4 x 11-inch painted paper strips. Follow directions on page 25 for the painted paper technique.

BASIC TECHNIQUES USED

Painted paper

Loose scroll

Shaping

INSTRUCTIONS

1

Photocopy the filliped alphabet pattern on page 120, reducing or enlarging as needed for your project. Alternatively, trace the letters desired. Place the letters under a sheet of clear acetate.

2

Review the instructions for making the letters on page 20. Using any width of paper desired, estimate the length of the strip needed for a letter, and cut to size. Make a very loose scroll by first rolling the paper tightly three or four times around the quilling tool, then unrolling and rerolling loosely with your fingers. Use this same technique for the curled ends of each letter. Shape curves with the handle of the slotted tool or a 1/8-inch dowel. Make tight curves by shaping around a toothpick or a similar-size tool. Many letters will consist of several pieces and shapes.

3

After all the letter pieces are finished, begin gluing the pieces together to make completed letters. Allow these to dry completely.

4

Arrange and glue the letters onto decorative background paper for framing. Display your monogram in a shadow box or in a frame without glass.

QUILLED CIRCLE ALPHABET

Quilled letters will make your scrapbook titles pop! They're so easy to make that you may find yourself writing entire journal entries with them or personalizing everything in sight.

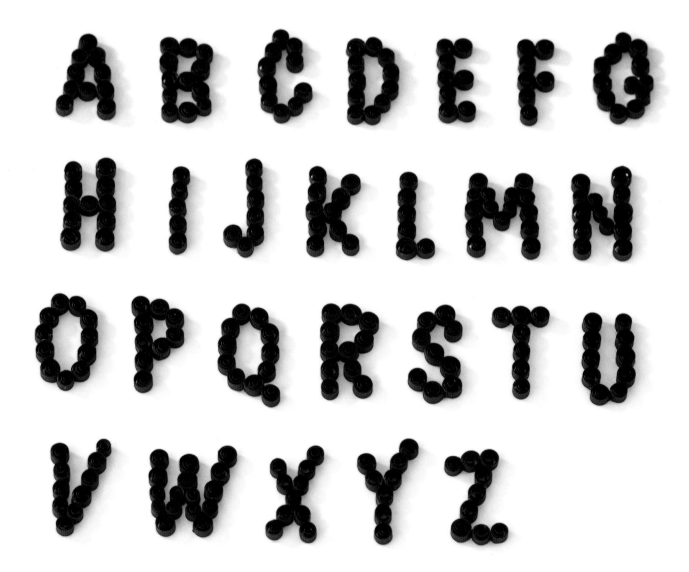

YOU WILL NEED

Basic quilling tool kit (page 8)

Photocopier or tracing paper

⅛-inch strips of paper

BASIC TECHNIQUE USED

Loose circle

INSTRUCTIONS

1

Photocopy the circle alphabet template on page 119, reducing or enlarging as needed for your project. Alternatively, you can simply trace the letters needed.

2

Tear ⅛-inch paper strips (your choice of color) into 2 ½-inch lengths. Roll these into loose circles that are all equal in size.

3

Place the alphabet pattern or traced letters under a piece of clear acetate. Apply a thin line of glue on the acetate, tracing the shape of the letter you're about to make. This will create a thin glue-back that will make the finished letter more durable. Using the pattern as a guide, glue loose circles to each other at the sides to form the letters as you place them on the acetate. Let dry.

TIP▶ • **Make up some phrases in advance and glue them to pieces of card stock: "FOR BABY" (use pastel colors to make the circles), "OVER THE HILL" (black letters), "HAPPY BIRTHDAY" (solid primary color letters), "BEE WELL" (black, white, and bright yellow letters), or "CONGRATS" (any festive color). Adhere the cards to the front of a plain paper bag for a unique last-minute gift decoration.**

FRAMED SOCCER MEMORY

Kick your scrapbook pages out of the album and into a frame! Use the loose circle alphabet to create a fresh, eye-catching (and dimensional) title. Add crimped paper strips to frame your photo and quill pentagons to embellish soccer ball stickers.

YOU WILL NEED

Basic quilling tool kit (page 8)

Photocopier or tracing paper

1/8-inch and 1/4-inch strips of paper

(colors to match soccer ball stickers)

Soccer ball stickers

Card stock (white and coordinating colors)

Adhesive tabs

Decorative scrapbooking paper, 12 x 12 inches

Photograph(s)

Embellishments (stickers,

journal blocks, statistics, etc.)

Paper crimper

Frame, 12 x 12 inches

BASIC TECHNIQUE USED

Loose circle

INSTRUCTIONS

1

Photocopy the circle alphabet pattern on page 119, reducing or enlarging as needed for your project. Alternatively, trace the letters for the word "soccer." Make the word by following the instructions on page 19 to make quilled circle letters, but don't make the letter O—you'll use a soccer ball sticker instead.

2

To make the pentagon shapes that are embellishing the soccer ball sticker, first cut 1/8-inch strips (in the same color as your soccer ball stickers) in half lengthwise to make 1/16-inch-wide paper. Tear strips into 6-inch lengths and roll these into loose circles. Glue down the loose end and allow to dry.

3

Pinch the sides of one circle to make five evenly spaced points and form a pentagon shape. Repeat with the rest of the circles.

4

Glue the circle letters made in step 1 to a piece of white card stock, using a soccer sticker for the letter O. Glue the pentagon shapes to the soccer sticker. Allow to dry.

5

Cut a rectangle around the word "soccer," then mat that onto a slightly larger card stock rectangle in a coordinating color. (See the photo.) Use the adhesive tabs to mount this on the decorative background paper.

6

Arrange photograph(s), journal blocks, statistics, etc., on your background page as desired, using colored card stock to mat items. Make square or rectangular frames by gluing the ends of crimped paper strips together at the corners, overlapping the ends before gluing. Mount all items to the background paper with adhesive tabs. If you like, place your finished page in a frame.

FUNKY FAUX FLOWERS

Go where no gardener has gone before! Quill a fantasy bouquet of colorful mums using your favorite colors—even if they can't be found in nature.

YOU WILL NEED

Basic quilling tool kit (page 8)

Double-sided medium-weight paper

(various colors)

Paper trimmer

Craft knife

Polystyrene foam packing peanuts

Covered wire floral stems

Double-sided adhesive dots

Floral tape

Photocopier or tracing paper

Green medium-weight paper

BASIC TECHNIQUES USED

Fringed flower with center (A)

Fringing (page 23)

A

INSTRUCTIONS

1

Refer to page 23 for instructions on making a fringed flower with a center. You'll use a variation of this technique and much wider and longer strips of paper to make the flowers in this project.

2

Trim four 2 x 11-inch strips and one 1/2 x 11-inch strip from a sheet of double-sided paper. Tear a 6-inch-long strip from the 1/2 x 11-inch strip and set it aside.

3

Glue the four 2-inch-wide strips together end-to-end to create a strip approximately 44 inches in length (overlap the ends just enough to glue them together). Choose the color you want the flower to be, and lay the long strip with your choice of color facing up.

4

Glue the 1/2 x 6-inch strip parallel to the top edge of the long strip on the left-hand side. This strip will form the center of your flower.

5

Fringe the entire length of the long strip. The cuts should be approximately 1/4 inch apart and should stop about 3/8 inch in from the top edge of the strip.

6

For a realistic mum effect, the fringe in the center of the flower should be shorter than the rest, so you'll need to diagonally trim the fringed edge of the first section (see figure).

To do so, first measure ¹/2 inch down from the top left edge of the first fringed section. Draw a diagonal line from there to the bottom right edge of that same section, then cut along this line with scissors.

7

Slightly moisten the end of the narrow strip to make starting easier. Begin quilling a fringed flower, carefully keeping the right side edge even as you roll tight. The flower center and the rolled unfringed edge will create a short flower base. Glue the end and let dry.

8

Spread the fringed pieces out and away from the center of the flower with your fingers. Beginning with the outer fringe, roll the ends toward the center of the flower using a toothpick. This process is time consuming, so curl as many or few as you desire, but be sure to curl a few of the shorter center fringe strips.

9

Use the craft knife to carve a cone shape from one packing peanut. Be careful—it's easy to cut yourself while doing this! Press the cone shape point-side-down onto a wire stem. Place a double-sided adhesive dot on the flat part of the cone and attach the base of the flower to it. Starting with the base of the flower, wrap the base, cone, and stem wire with floral tape.

10

Photocopy or trace the leaf pattern on page 117. Use this to cut two leaves from the green paper. Use the floral tape to attach the stems of the leaves to the flower stem.

TIP▸● If you're making a large bouquet of flowers, cut and glue all of your strips first. Then you can fringe and curl all the blooms while watching a favorite television show or movie. Or ask the kids or a friend to help. Many hands make light work!

MIDNIGHT AT THE OASIS

*Surely you remember the lyrics: "Send your camel to bed,
shadows paintin' our faces, traces of romance in our heads."
Even if you don't remember the words, this cleverly quilled image
of a desert oasis is a soothing sight at the end of a long day.*

YOU WILL NEED

Basic quilling tool kit (page 8)

¹/₈-inch-wide paper strips (brown)

¹/₄-inch-wide paper strips (tan)

¹/₂-inch-wide strips of green paper*

Decorative paper in sunset colors,

12 x 12-inches

Heavily textured sand-colored paper

or sandpaper

Frame, 6 x 12 inches

* Use medium-thick handmade paper for the leaves. The easier the paper tears, the easier it will be to fringe.

BASIC TECHNIQUES USED

Loose circle (A)

Square (B)

Fringing (page 23)

Double fringing (C)

Tight bullet (D)

Semiloose circle (peg) (E)

A   B

C

D   E

INSTRUCTIONS

1

To begin making the trunks, tear four 5-inch strips, nine 4-inch strips, seven 3-inch strips, and four 2-inch strips from the ¹/₈-inch-wide brown paper. Roll the strips into loose circles, then shape them into squares.

2

Stack the squares as shown in the photo to create the tree trunks. Place the largest squares at the bottom, the smallest squares at the top. Make three trunks of different heights. Glue the squares together to form curved trunks as you work. Set aside and let dry.

3

To begin making the palm fronds, tear ten 6-inch strips, ten 5-inch strips, and five 4-inch strips from the ¹/₂-inch-wide green paper. Use a pointy object (such as the end of a quilling tool) and a ruler to score down the center of each strip lengthwise. Fold the strips in half along the scored line, then cut one end of each strip in a curving diagonal line.

4

Unfold a strip and fringe the frond, one side at a time. Fringe at a 45 degree angle away from the pointed end, almost to the center fold, spacing the cuts approximately $1/16$ inch apart.

5

After all the fronds are fringed, fold each in half at the score and fringe again in the same direction. This double-fringing technique creates a more feathery effect.

6

To make the coconuts, tear $1/4$-inch strips of tan paper into six 3-inch lengths. Cut each in half diagonally, from one corner to the opposite corner, to make 12 long triangles. Make tight bullets with 8 of these triangles. (A slotted quilling tool is suggested for this technique.) Begin rolling tightly at the wide end of the strip. Glue the roll at the pointed end.

7

Use three of the four remaining triangles to make smaller tight bullets. (Discard the remaining triangle.) To do so, first shorten each triangle's length by tearing $1/2$ inch off the end opposite the point. Then roll three tight bullets as described in step 6.

8

Make three semiloose circle pegs using a 12-inch, a 10-inch, and an 8-inch strip of $1/4$-inch tan paper. Set these aside.

9

To begin assembling the pieces, first lay the quilled trunks on your work surface. Arrange six of the smallest fronds on the shortest trunk. Overlap the fronds to obtain the effect desired.

Use the longer fronds on the larger trunks. You can vary the length of the fronds for the taller trees by tearing a bit off of the straight ends. When the fronds are arranged to your liking, glue the square ends together at the center. Let them dry.

10

Glue three large coconuts to the center of the largest set of fronds and three more to the next largest. Glue the smallest coconuts to the smallest fronds. Glue the tan circle pegs to the back of the assembled fronds.

11

Cut a 6 x 12-inch piece of the sunset paper for the background. Tear about 10 pieces of different sizes from the sand-colored paper or sandpaper. Glue the sand pieces to the background, overlapping to create the desert floor. Insert the background into the frame.

12

Arrange the tree trunks and frond clusters on the background as desired. First, glue the trunks in place; top each trunk with a group of fronds. Let the glue dry, then shape and bend the individual fronds as desired.

HARLEQUIN COASTERS

The classic black and white harlequin pattern is given a southwestern twist with these desert-toned colors. If this palette isn't what you desire, pair lime green with orange for a summery look— or shades of azure and aquamarine to remind you of the deep blue sea.

YOU WILL NEED

Basic quilling tool kit (page 8)

¹/₄-inch-wide paper strips (turquoise, tan, and copper)

Copper-leaf pen

Decorative background paper to match your color scheme

Double-sided adhesive tape

3 x 3-inch plastic square coaster (available in craft stores or online)

BASIC TECHNIQUES USED

Loose circle (A)

Square shape (B)

Diamond shape (C)

Tight circle (peg) (D)

INSTRUCTIONS

1

Tear fourteen 6-inch-long turquoise strips. Roll these into 14 loose circles approximately ³/₈ inch in diameter. Tear fourteen 6-inch-long tan strips. Roll these into 14 loose circles approximately ³/₈ inch in diameter.

2

Shape all of these loose circles into squares. Pinch two opposite corners of each square slightly to make a diamond shape. Set all 28 of these diamond shapes aside.

3

Tear the copper paper into 35 strips that are 3 inches in length. Roll these into tight circle pegs

that are ¹/₈ inch in diameter. Smooth out the top of each peg by applying pressure with the flat end of a slotted quilling tool or a dowel. Color the top of each peg with the copper-leaf pen.

4

The design is made up of four horizontal rows (with seven diamond shapes in each row) separated by copper-leafed pegs. Alternate the colors of diamond shapes—if one row starts with a turquoise diamond, start the next row with a tan diamond. To begin making the first row, glue the side points of seven diamonds together with dots of glue. Once the row is done, glue a tight roll peg to the top and bottom points of each diamond shape.

5

Attach a second row of diamond shapes, adding diamonds one at a time by gluing the bottom points to the pegs and side points to each other. When you've completed the second row of diamonds, glue a peg to the top of each diamond, then continue adding rows of diamonds and pegs in this manner until you have four rows of diamonds and five rows of pegs. Allow the glue to dry.

6

Using the packaging insert in the coaster as a template, cut out a same-size piece from the decorative paper. Attach this decorative paper to the coaster insert with the tape. Center and glue the harlequin design onto the decorative paper. Once the glue has dried, insert the design inside the coaster.

A

B

C

D

LONGEVITY SEAL

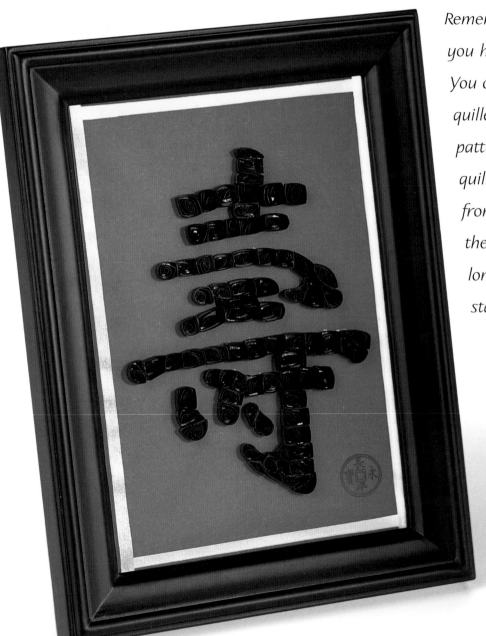

Remember how much fun you had with coloring books? You can use almost any quilled shape to fill in any pattern. Use your favorite quilled shapes—all formed from loose circles—to create the Chinese ideogram for longevity. Just be sure to stay inside the lines!

YOU WILL NEED

Basic quilling tool kit (page 8)

1/8-inch-wide paper strips (black)

Longevity pattern (page 122)

Photocopier or tracing paper

Red vellum

Frame

Gold-leaf pen or strips of gold paper

Chinese coin stamp

Permanent black ink pad

Easel (optional)

BASIC TECHNIQUES USED

Loose circle (A)

Square (B)

Teardrop (C)

Shaped teardrop (D)

Marquise (E)

Shaped marquise (F)

Crescent (G))

INSTRUCTIONS

1

Tear about eighty 2- to 4-inch-long black strips. Roll the strips into loose circles of various sizes.

2

Photocopy or trace the longevity pattern on page 122. Place the pattern under a sheet of acetate. Begin filling in the pattern by determining the sizes and shapes of pieces needed as you work (use the loose circles you've already rolled, shaping them as needed). Place the shapes on the acetate to fill in the pattern.

3

When you're satisfied with one section, glue the quilled shapes together and let them dry. When you've completed the entire pattern, let all the sections dry.

4

Cut the red vellum to fit inside your frame and then embellish the edges with the gold-leaf pen or thin strips of gold paper. Let dry. Remove the pattern from under the acetate, and center the red vellum (you'll be able to see through it) on top of it.

5

Pry the glued sections off the acetate with your quilling tool. Glue each section in place on the red vellum and let them dry.

6

Add a decorative touch to the lower corner using the coin stamp and black ink. Put your completed project in the frame and display on an easel if desired.

TIP▶ • This same "fill in the blank" technique can be used with coloring book drawings, quilt patterns, kaleidoscope patterns, or clip art to create your own special quilled images.

A

B

C

D

E

F   G

POTTED POSIES

These potted posy pins are perfect wardrobe

pick-me-ups that can be worn year-round.

Try saying that nine times in a row.

YOU WILL NEED

Basic quilling tool kit (page 8)

1/4-inch-wide paper strips (green, tan, and various shades of pink and lavender)

Decoupage scissors (or fringing tool)

Wire cutters

Craft wire, 24-gauge green

Split wooden flowerpot, 2 inches tall (available at craft stores)

Card stock

1-inch foam ball

Craft knife

Gold acrylic paint

Paintbrush

Pin back, 1 inch

BASIC TECHNIQUES USED

Chalking (page 25)

Fringed flower with center (A)

Loose scroll (curl) (B)

Tight roll (C)

Small bullet (D)

A

C

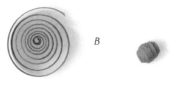

B

D

INSTRUCTIONS

NOTE▶• The instructions below are for the gold flowerpot with the gerbers; instructions for the variation (red flowerpot with the daisies) follow.

1

Fringe a 1/4 x 3-inch strip of pink or lavender paper, using decoupage scissors (or fringing tool). Glue a 1/8 x 2-inch strip of the same color paper to the top right of the fringed strip with fringe on the left side. (This narrower, unfringed strip will form the flower's center.) Using a slotted tool, start rolling tightly at the end of the unfringed strip. When finished rolling, apply only a small dot of glue to the loose end before gluing to the side. Spread the fringe outward away from the center of the flower with your fingernail. Make 15 of these gerber daisies. Optional: Make 15 small bullets from eight 1-inch strips and glue to centers.

2

Make a tight roll from a 1/8 x 1-inch strip of green paper. Glue to the back of the fringed flower for the stem holder. Wrap a 2-inch piece of green wire around a toothpick to form a spiral, keeping 1/4 inch of each end straight. Stretch the spiral to 1 1/4 inches in length. Glue one end into the stem holder of the flower.

3

Cut a 1/8 x 12-inch strip of tan paper in half lengthwise. Tear the 1/16-inch-wide strips into 1/2-inch-long pieces. Roll the pieces into loose curls and make a pile of about 25 for the flowerpot soil. Set aside.

4

Lay the flowerpot flat on the card stock and trace around the shape with a pencil. Cut around the shape inside the line and set aside. Cut the foam ball in half with a craft knife. Push the rounded side of the half into the lower bottom portion of the flowerpot. Cut the remaining piece of foam ball in half again, and glue one foam wedge in the back of the flowerpot on top of the other piece. Push the foam pieces down so there is at least 1/8 inch of space below the top of the flowerpot. Press the flowerpot face-up on a flat surface to ensure the back is flat. Glue the card stock shape to the back of the flowerpot.

5

Paint the pot with gold acrylic paint and allow it to dry overnight.

6

Lay the flowerpot on a flat surface and insert the flowers into the foam. Make a row in the back and add flowers to the sides. Insert the remaining flowers in front. Hold the flowerpot upright and fill the top portion with glue almost to the top. Use a toothpick to spread the glue around evenly. Add the loose curls for soil. Use tweezers to fill in blank spots with curls. (Make additional curls if necessary.) Prop the flowerpot upright and let dry overnight.

7

Once everything is dry, you can shape and arrange the flowers. For the flowers on the back row, hold the base of each flower stem with tweezers and pull up on the flower to lengthen the stem. Add more curls if needed.

8

Glue the pin back to the upper portion of the flowerpot and allow to dry completely.

VARIATION▸● To make the daisies in the red flowerpot instead, follow the directions above but use 1/4 x 4-inch strips of fringed white paper for the petals and a 1/8 x 2 1/2-inch strip of bright yellow paper for the center. Use green paper for the twenty-five 1/16 x 1/2-inch curls (the soil). Paint the flowerpot with red acrylic paint.

TRÈS CHIC TRIO OF DRESSES

These gowns are fast and easy (no glued ends!). Fill in the patterns
with the colors of your own dressy desires. And remember:
Every elegant wardrobe can use just one little black dress.

YOU WILL NEED

Basic quilling tool kit (page 8)

White matte card stock

1/8-inch-wide paper strips (your choice of colors)

Dry-embossing tool

Dress templates (see page 116)

Fine-point gold opaque paint marker

Chalk (colors should match paper strips)

Acid-free spray fixative

Matted gold picture frame

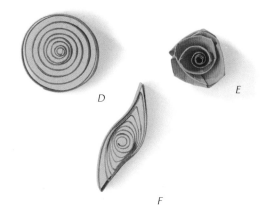

BASIC TECHNIQUES USED

S scroll (A)

C scroll (B)

Loose scroll (C)

Loose circle (D)

Folded rose (E)

Shaped marquise (F)

Chalking (page 25)

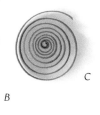

INSTRUCTIONS

1

Trim a piece of card stock to fit your frame. Dry-emboss a dress design in the center using one of the dress templates on pages 116 and 117.

2

Use the embossing tool to draw the hanger and add dots along the hem of the dress. Highlight the hanger and dots with the gold paint pen.

3

Using the same color of chalk as the paper strips, lightly outline the edges of the dress. For added dimension, chalk the inside edge of the frame's mat with the same shade.

4

Use ⅛-inch-wide strips of paper in lengths varying from ½ to 1¼ inches to make a variety of simple shapes. Begin by making mostly S scrolls, C scrolls, and loose scrolls from ¾- to 1-inch-long strips. Unroll the loose scrolls slightly to create a tail. Also make a number of ½-inch loose circles rolled tightly and left unglued.

5

Place the shapes randomly inside the outlined dress, but don't glue them yet. The S scrolls work well to outline the pattern. Fill in the dress with the remaining shapes. The ½-inch loose circles fit well in small areas such as the straps of the dresses. Place a small folded rose at the waist of one of the dresses.

6

When you're pleased with how the dress looks, use the tweezers to pick up the individual shapes and glue them down one at a time. Put a small puddle of glue on a piece of acetate, and as you pick up the shapes, lightly dip them in the glue—only a touch is needed. Begin at the top of the dress with the smallest shapes and work down from the waist. Try to keep the pieces evenly spaced and not too bunched up. Let dry.

7

Place the chalked mat over the decorated card stock. Cover your work surface with waxed paper and set your matted artwork on it. Spray lightly with an acid-free spray fixative to set the chalk and prevent smearing. Sign your work with a small quilled initial, then place in a frame.

TIP ▶ • Know when to stop filling in the shapes. Too many pieces bunched up will take away from the intricate, scrolled appearance of the dress.

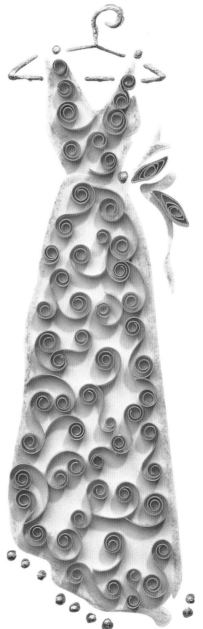

WHIMSICAL BUTTERFLY SHELF

Set a flock of colorful quilled butterflies aflutter on a wooden shelf. Sweet and simple, it will add a touch of whimsy to any little girl's room. Make additional butterflies for matching picture frames and other room accessories.

YOU WILL NEED

Basic quilling tool kit (page 8)

¹/₄-inch-wide paper strips

(five shades of pastel colors)

Paper crimper

Small half-pearls

Wooden shelf, painted color of your choice

BASIC TECHNIQUES USED

Looping (see illustration)

Loose circle (A)

Teardrop (B)

Marquise (C)

V scroll (D)

Note: Crimp all paper after measuring, except the 2-inch strip for the head.

INSTRUCTIONS

1

This project calls for making seven to nine butterflies in various shades. For each butterfly, tear two ¹/₄ x 12-inch strips for the top wings. Make a ¹/₄-inch fold to begin looping. Make six loops, allowing a bit more space between each loop as the loops get bigger. Glue the end of the strip at the bottom of the loop and tear off any excess.

2

Repeat this to make the other wing, but compare the size of the second wing to the first before gluing. If the second looped wing is obviously not the same size, re-crimp the strip and start over.

3

Hold the glued end of a wing in one hand and flatten the strip to a point with your thumb and index fingers. Push the point in toward the center to make the top wing shape. Repeat this process to shape the second wing.

4

Tear two ¹/₄ x 6-inch strips for the bottom wings. Make a loose circle approximately ⁵/₈ inch in diameter and shape it into a teardrop. Make the second bottom wing the same size and shape.

5

Tear a ¹/₄ x 6-inch strip and roll it into a loose circle ³/₄ inch in diameter. Shape the loose circle into a marquise and flatten it slightly, making it approximately 1 inch in length for the body.

6

Roll a loose circle with a ¹/₄ x 2-inch strip for the head. Then make a V scroll for the antenna using a ¹/₄ x 2-inch black strip.

7

Arrange all the butterfly parts, then glue them together using the photo as a guide. Glue a half-pearl embellishment on top of the head. Let dry, then use all-purpose glue to attach the butterflies to the face of the shelf in a random design.

A

B

C

D

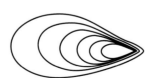

CARMEN MIRANDA MAGNETS

Face facts: No one has enough fridge magnets for all those tedious lists or treasured snapshots. Give your refrigerator and kitchen a bright, boom-chicka-boom with these juicy quilled fruit magnets.

YOU WILL NEED

Basic quilling tool kit (page 8)

¼-inch-wide paper strips (various colors, see instructions)

Paper crimper

Card stock (in colors to match fruits)

Chalk (brown, yellow, red, and black)

Medium-weight bright green paper

1-inch dowel (a jumbo marker or utensil handle will work)

Magnets, extra strong

Acid-free spray fixative

BASIC TECHNIQUES USED

Chalking (page 25)

Semitight circle (A)

Loose circle (B)

Shaped marquise (C)

Teardrop (D)

Spiral

Marquise (E)

Crescent (F)

Note: Crimp all paper strips in this project prior to quilling, except where noted. Quilling instructions are given for each fruit, and instructions for turning the fruits into magnets follow at the end.

ORANGE

1

Glue six ¼ x 12-inch strips of orange paper end-to-end to make a 72-inch strip. Roll this into a semitight circle. Place the circle on a flat surface, release the tension to 1½ inches in diameter, and glue the loose end.

2

When gluing the fruit shape to the orange card stock back (see assembly instructions), use the tweezers to pull the center coil up and off-center. Apply brown chalk around the center coil to make an orange navel.

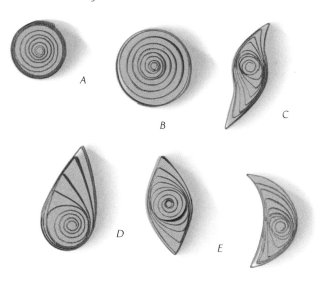

APPLE

1

Glue six ¼ x 12-inch strips of red paper end-to-end to make a 72-inch strip. Roll it into a semitight circle. Place the circle on a flat surface, release the tension to 1½ inches in diameter, and glue the loose end.

2

Press the top of the shape against a pencil to form an indention. Press near the bottom on both sides to make a slight point. Press up on the point once to complete the shape.

3

To make the stem, tear a ¼ x 4-inch strip of brown paper and roll it into a loose circle. Shape the loose circle into a stem.

4

To make the leaves, tear two ¼ x 10-inch strips of the bright green paper. Roll each into a loose circle, then pinch each into a shaped marquise.

5

When gluing the apple to red card stock (see assembly instructions), use the tweezers to pull the center coil up and to the right. To add the shine effect, apply yellow chalk halfway around the center coil in a moon shape. Glue the stem and two leaves to the top of the apple.

GRAPES

1

Make the following quilled shapes: 14 loose circles from ¼ x 4-inch purple strips, one shaped stem from a ¼ x 4-inch brown strip, two teardrops from ¼ x 6-inch olive green strips, and three shaped marquises from ¼ x 3-inch olive green strips.

2

Cut a ¼ x 3-inch strip of brown paper lengthwise. Do not crimp these two pieces, but shape them into two spirals.

3

Using the photo as a guide, arrange the pieces and glue them together on a piece of card stock (see assembly instructions).

PLUM

1

Glue four ¼ x 12-inch purple strips end-to-end to make a 48-inch strip. Roll this into a semitight circle.

2

Place the circle on a flat surface, release the tension to 1 3/8 inches in diameter, and glue the loose end. Push in the sides to make an egg shape.

3

Make the leaf by quilling a ¼ x 8-inch olive green strip into a marquise. Make the stem by loosely folding a ¼ x 3-inch olive green strip.

4

When gluing the shape to the purple card stock back (see assembly instructions), use the tweezers to pull the center coil down toward the wider end of the egg shape. Glue the stem and leaf to the top of the plum.

PEAR

1

Glue six ¼ x 12-inch yellow strips end-to-end to make a 72-inch strip. Roll into a semitight circle.

2

Place the circle on a flat surface, release the tension to 1½ inches in diameter, and glue the loose end.

3

Shape into a pear by curling the sides at the top around a 1-inch dowel—be careful not to make the top pointed. Quill a ¼ x 6-inch olive green strip into a marquise for a leaf. Make a stem by loosely folding a ¼ x 5-inch brown paper strip.

4

When gluing the pear shape to the yellow card stock back (see assembly instructions), use the tweezers to pull the center coil down and off-center. Apply red chalk vertically on one side. Glue the stem and leaf to the top of the pear.

BANANA

1

Glue six ¼ x 12-inch yellow strips end-to-end to make a 72-inch strip. Roll this into a semitight circle.

2

Place the circle on a flat surface, release the tension to 2 inches in diameter, and glue the loose end.

3

Use the dowel to shape this into a crescent. Make a slight point on one end and a squared point on the other.

4

When gluing to the yellow card stock back (see assembly instructions), use the tweezers to pull the center coil up and off-center. Apply black chalk halfway up on one side.

ASSEMBLY

1

After shaping each fruit, place it on a piece of matching card stock and trace around the design with a pencil. Cut out the shape inside the line to make it slightly smaller than the quilled shape.

2

Follow the instructions that were given in the individual instructions for gluing the fruit shape to the card stock.

3

After attaching the fruit shape to the card stock, use all-purpose glue to add a strong magnet to the back of each piece.

4

Place the fruit magnets face-up on a sheet of waxed paper and spray them lightly with the fixative to set the chalk and prevent smearing.

DOUBLE-QUILLED BROOCHES

Give in to the temptation to make one of these brooches for every ensemble you own. Double quilling uses two colors of paper to add even more visual interest to simple shapes. Use contrasting or complementary colors or a simple combination of black and white— the choice is yours.

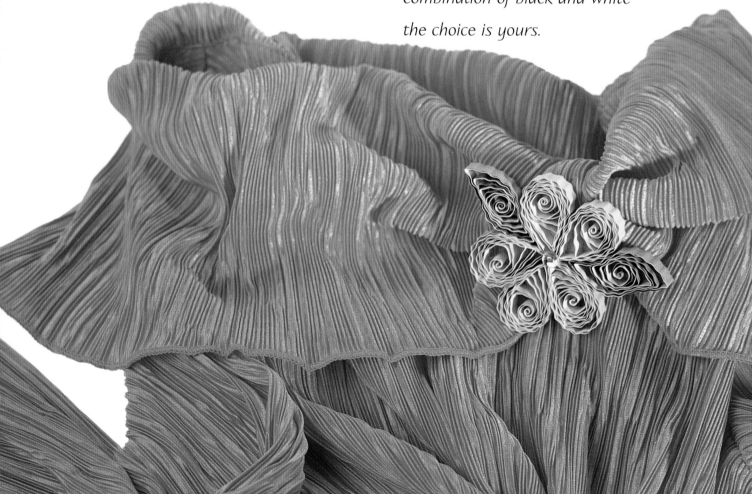

YOU WILL NEED

Basic quilling tool kit (page 8)

3/8-inch-wide paper strips (various colors)

Paper crimper

Rhinestone, pearl, or bead for brooch center

Card stock (in matching color)

1-inch metal bar pin

BASIC TECHNIQUES USED

Double quilling (page 24)

Loose circle (A)

Teardrop (B)

Shaped marquise (C)

A

B

C

INSTRUCTIONS

1

Tear five 3/8 x 11 1/2-inch strips of one color—these will be the outer strips of paper that form the petals. Tear five 3/8 x 9 1/2-inch strips of a contrasting or complementary color—these will be the inner strips of paper that form the petals. Follow the instructions for double quilling on page 24 to attach the strips together to create five double strips. Let dry. Before rolling the double strips, use the crimper to crimp each set of two strips.

2

Referring to the instructions on page 000 again, roll each double strip into a loose circle approximately 1 inch in diameter. Trim off any of the inner strip that extends past the outer strip when done rolling, and glue the end of outer strip in place. Allow to dry. Pinch into teardrop shapes. Make five teardrop shapes in all.

3

To make the leaves, tear two 3/8 x 12-inch green outer strips and two 3/8 x 10 x 1/2-inch lighter green inner strips. Glue together, allow to dry, and crimp. Roll these into two loose circles approximately 1 1/4 inch in diameter. Pinch each circle into a shaped marquise.

4

Glue the teardrops together at the points to form a flower. Glue the shaped-marquise leaves between two petals, as shown. Glue a rhinestone or other embellishment to the flower center. Let dry.

5

Cut out a 1-1/2-inch-diameter circle from the matching card stock. Glue it to the center back of brooch. Glue the bar pin horizontally at the top of the circle backing and allow it to dry overnight.

BOUQUETIÈRE

A Parisian flower seller would feel right at home with the pale blue striping, elegant white wirework, and dainty blossoms of this miniature shadowbox. If you've always wanted to create a miniature world with paper, this is the project to try.

YOU WILL NEED

*Basic quilling tool kit (page 8)**

Hand punch, ¹/₄-inch flower shape

Dry-embossing tool

(for forming punched flowers)

Small square of craft foam

Wire cutters

Covered floral wire, green

¹/₈-inch-wide strips

(various colors, see instructions)

Dowels, various sizes

Craft wire, 32 gauge

1-inch foam ball

Color chalk (yellow, orange and red)

Paper punches, small ash, oak, and birch leaves

Paper punch, ¹/₂-inch circle

Book board, 1 x 3 x ¹/₈ inches

Craft knife

Rotary cutter

White craft box

Decorative paper

(we used blue and white pinstripe)

Sheet of white paper

Decorative-edge scissors

* Tweezers are a MUST for this project!

BASIC TECHNIQUES USED

Chalking (page 25)

Punched flower (page 22)

Semitight circle (A)

Square (B)

Tight circle (C)

Fringing (page 23)

Loose scroll (curl) (D)

S scroll (E)

Fringed flower with center (page 23)

Punched leaves

Folded rose (F)

Loops (G)

Loose circle (H)

Open heart scroll (I)

V scroll (J)

Note: Instructions are given first for making the plants and containers as shown from left to right in the photo. Instructions for making the shadow box plant shop follow.

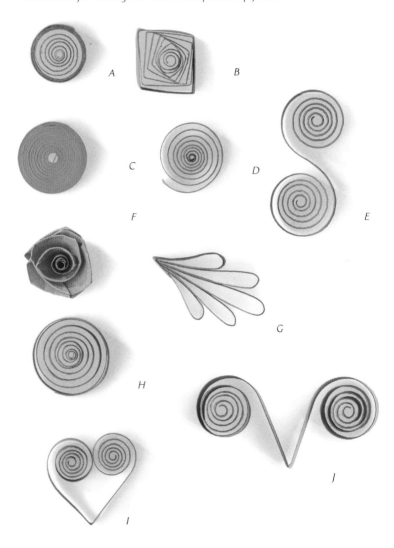

INSTRUCTIONS

DELPHINIUMS

1

See page 22 for instructions for making punched flowers. Punch a pile of 1/4-inch flowers in one color (purple, lavender, or white). When the tiny flower is shaped, its center forms a sort of point with six petals. Glue one petal of each of two shaped flowers together. After you've done this you should be able to see where two petals on a third flower will fit between the two glued flowers. Glue this third flower on to make a bloom. Make at least two dozen of these blooms in the three colors to start.

2

Cut three pieces of floral wire 1 1/4, 1 1/2, and 1 3/4 inches long. Cover all the wire except 1/2 inch at the bottom with these blooms. Start at the top of the wire and work down. Two flower petals of each bloom will fit perfectly on the wire. Turn the wire slightly as you glue. When all the flowers are dry, bend the stems and shape them as you arrange them in the container. Make three of each color.

DELPHINIUM CONTAINER

1

Make the following shapes using 1/8-inch white strips of paper. Glue 12-inch strips end-to-end to the lengths specified:

Square: Roll a semitight circle 3/4 inch in diameter using a 24-inch strip of paper. Shape into a square.

Small square: Roll a semitight circle 5/8 inch in diameter using a 20-inch strip of paper. Shape into a square.

Round dome: Roll a 24-inch strip around a 3/16-inch dowel (the size of a metal slotted tool handle) three or four times, then slip off the dowel. Continue rolling with your fingers and make a tight circle. Use your thumbs to shape the circle into a bowl. Spread glue on the inside with a toothpick to retain the shape.

Connector: Roll a 4-inch strip around a 3/16-inch dowel to make a tight circle. Slip the roll off the dowel and glue down the loose end.

Small round dome: Roll a tight circle using a 24-inch strip of paper. Use your thumbs to shape the circle into a bowl. Spread glue on the inside with a toothpick to retain the shape.

Pedestal vase: Roll a 36-inch strip around a 3/16-inch dowel three or four times, then slip off the dowel. Continue rolling with your fingers to make a tight circle. Lay the tight circle on a hard, flat surface; press around the circle to flatten it. Use your thumbs to shape it into a tall vase. Spread glue on the inside with a toothpick to retain the shape.

2

Allow all pieces to dry completely. Starting with the square shape on the bottom, glue the shapes together on top of one another in the order made. (Use the photo for reference.) Make sure the glued seams on all pieces are lined up as you glue. When dry, arrange the blooms in the pedestal.

FERN

1

Use ¼-inch-wide green strips cut to 2-, 1 ¾-, and 1-½-inch lengths for the fern. Use a pointy object (such as the end of a quilling tool) and a ruler to score down the center of each strip length-wise. Fold the strips in half along the scored line, then trim the top end of each strip into a curved point.

2

Fringe each strip at an angle toward the pointed end. Cut almost to the fold as you fringe, fringing to within ⅜ inch of the end of each strip. Make as many fronds as needed to fill the container. Fringe a dozen or so shorter pieces to glue around the outer edge.

FERN CONTAINER

1

Roll a 144-inch strip of white paper around a ³/₁₆-inch dowel three or four times, then slip off the dowel. Continue rolling with your fingers to make a tight circle.

2

Lay the tight circle on a hard, flat surface; press around the circle to flatten it. Use your thumbs and a rounded object to shape it into a flat-bottom container (see photo).

3

Spread glue on the inside with a toothpick to retain the shape. As the glue is drying, place a dozen or so ¼ x ¾-inch loose scrolls (made from the same green paper as the ferns) into the container. This paper-fill will make it easier to glue the fern leaves into the container. Add the ferns.

WROUGHT IRON FERN STAND

1

The stand is made with 32-gauge wire glued between two strips of ⅛-inch-wide white paper. Tear twelve 4-inch strips of ⅛-inch-wide paper, and cut six 4-inch pieces of wire. Straighten the wire and glue each piece between two strips. (This can be a tedious process, so take your time—it will be worth it.) Allow all pieces to dry.

2

The scrolls range from 1 to 4 inches. Set aside three of the paper/wire pieces to use for the three legs (S scrolls). Cut the remaining 4-inch wire strips to the lengths needed, using the illustration for lengths and making the specific shapes for one leg. Shape the scrolls around dowels of all sizes. Make additional paper/wire strips if needed.

3

Trim the ends of the scrolls when they're completed. Glue the shapes together to make a leg. Make all three legs exactly the same for this plant stand.

4

Make the round top of the stand by wrapping a $^1/_8$ x 2$^1/_2$-inch strip of wire paper around a $^3/_4$-inch dowel. Overlap the end slightly and glue down.

5

Apply glue to the top of the three S scrolls where the round top touches, and glue the circle top in place. Glue the lower portion of the S scroll legs where they touch. When dry, place the plant stand on a flat surfaceand make any adjustments to ensure the plant stand is level and straight.

6

Place the container of fern on the top of the stand and glue in place.

MINIATURE GERBER DAISIES

1

Fringe one $^1/_8$ x 2-inch pink strip (this will form one flower's petals). Cut a $^1/_8$ x 1-inch light green strip in half lengthwise. One of these $^1/_{16}$-inch light green strips will be used for the flower center; set the other one aside to roll into a stem holder.

2

Glue the $^1/_{16}$ x 1-inch center strip to the top right of the fringed strip with the fringe on the left side. Using a slotted tool, start rolling tightly, beginning with the $^1/_{16}$-inch strip. Apply only a small dot of glue to attach the loose end. Spread the fringe away from the center of the flower with your fingernail.

3

Roll a tight circle with the remaining $^1/_{16}$-inch strip to make a stem holder. Glue this on the back of the flower. Allow all the flowers to dry; then glue a 1$^1/_2$- length of covered floral wire in the stem holder.

4

Repeat steps 1 through 3 to make more flowers. Our bouquet consists of three pink flowers with light green centers, three gold with brown centers, four hot pink with yellow-green centers, and five orange with black centers.

MINIATURE GERBER DAISY CONTAINER

1

Roll a $^1/_4$ x 96-inch strip of white paper around a $^1/_2$-inch dowel three or four times, then slip off the dowel. Continue rolling with your fingers to make a tight circle.

2

Lay the tight circle on a hard, flat surface. Press around the circle to flatten it. The diameter should be slightly more than 1 inch. Now use your thumbs to shape it into a 1$^1/_2$-inch-tall container, as shown in the photo.

3

Spread glue on the inside with a toothpick to retain the shape. While the glue is still wet, cut approximately $^1/_3$ inch from a 1-inch foam ball with a craft knife. Drop the ball into the flower container with the flat side up. Let the container dry completely; place the fringed flowers into the container with a little of the wire stems showing. (If you can still see the foam ball after all the flowers are arranged, tear two $1/8$ x 12-inch strips of brown paper into $1/2$-inch pieces. Make loose scrolls with the strips and use tweezers to place them over the foam.)

FAUX STEMS

1

Cut twelve $1/16$ x 4-inch strips, using five colors (brown, green, tan, ivory, and coral). Curl the ends by placing the slotted tool $1/4$ inch from the strip's tip and turning it six times. Remove the tool and straighten out the curl so it's a spiral. Tear off $1/4$ to $1/2$ inch from a few of the stems to make various lengths.

FAUX STEM CONTAINER

1

Cut a 2 $1/2$ x 5-inch piece from a white sheet of paper. Roll the paper around a $1/2$-inch dowel to make a 2 $1/2$-inch-tall cylinder shape. Glue the edge down and slip the shape off the dowel. Punch a $1/2$-inch circle from the remaining paper, and glue to the bottom. Glue

three $1/8$ x 4-inch strips of white paper around the top of the cylinder, spaced apart, as shown in the photo. Place the stems in the container and arrange.

DISH GARDEN

1

Cut ten 1 1/2-inch-long slivers of 1/8-inch-wide green strips. Tear bits from the ends to make various lengths. Cut three more slivers from brown strips. Curl 1/4-inch of the pointed tips with your fingernail. Set aside.

2

Punch three ash leaves from a darker shade of green paper. Lightly chalk the leaf edges with yellow, orange, and red chalk.

3

Punch three flowers from white paper. Shape in the palm of your hand. Make three flower centers by rolling $1/16$ x $3/4$-inch white strips into tight circles. Glue one in the center of each shaped flower.

4

Punch six ash leaves from dark green paper. Snip off the top leaf and stem from each and discard the remaining pieces. Glue two leaves together at the stems. Repeat with the remaining four leaves. Glue one white shaped flower on top of each set of double leaves.

5

Punch five small oak leaves from a light shade of green.

DISH GARDEN CONTAINER

1

Roll a 144-inch strip of white paper around a $3/16$-inch dowel three or four times, then slip it off the dowel. Continue rolling with your fingers to make a tight circle. Lay the tight circle on a hard, flat surface and press around the circle to flatten it. Use your thumbs and a rounded object to shape the circle into a flat-bottom container (see the photo).

2

Spread glue on the inside with a toothpick to retain the shape. While the glue is drying inside, place a dozen or so $1/4$ x $1/2$-inch brown loose scrolls into the container. Make enough additional $1/8$ x $1/2$-inch dark green and light green curls to fill up the container to $1/4$ inch below the rim. Using the photo as a guide, arrange the plants in the dish garden. Glue in place.

NOTE▶● **Make the container for the roses first, then make the roses.**

ROSE CONTAINER

1

Roll a 144-inch white strip around a $3/16$-inch dowel three or four

times, then slip it off the dowel. Continue rolling with your fingers to make a tight circle.

2

Lay the tight roll on a hard, flat surface; press around the circle to flatten it. Use your thumbs and a rounded object to shape the circle into a bowl with a round bottom (see the photo). Spread glue on the inside with a toothpick to retain the shape. While the glue is drying inside, place a 1-inch foam ball inside the container. Let dry.

3

Roll a 60-inch white strip around a $3/16$-inch dowel three or four times, then slip it off the dowel. Continue rolling with your fingers to make a tight circle. Lay the tight roll on a hard, flat surface; press around the circle to flatten it. Glue it to the bottom of the bowl made in the previous step.

RED ROSES

1

Use $1/8$ x $3 1/2$-inch and $1/8$ x $4 1/2$-inch red strips to make the folded roses (see page 21). Using a slotted tool, roll a red strip three times for the rose's center, fold the paper, and make three complete turns, folding the strip with each turn. Continue making one-half turns and folding, making a total of seven to nine turns. Trim the end of the strip at an angle and glue to the side.

2

Repeat step 1 to make 15 to 20 roses. Glue the roses all over the top of the foam ball. Punch 25 birch leaves from green paper. Place most of them

between the container rim and the roses, but glue a few between roses if needed to hide the foam ball.

3

To make the single rose, glue one rose to a 1$\frac{1}{2}$-inch piece of covered floral wire. Punch out five birch leaves and glue them at the top of the stem under the rose. Place the single rose on the bench next to the container of roses.

WROUGHT IRON BENCH

1

Cut a 1 x 3 x $\frac{1}{8}$-inch rectangle from a piece of book board, using a ruler and craft knife. Make lattice by gluing $\frac{1}{8}$-inch white strips diagonally across the top and crisscrossing a second layer. When complete, turn the top over and trim the edges with the craft knife. Cover around the edge with a $\frac{1}{8}$ x 8-inch strip of white paper.

2

Use covered wire to make the S scrolls depicting wrought iron as described in the wrought iron fern stand instructions. The S scrolls range from 1 to 3$\frac{1}{2}$ inches. Tear twelve 4-inch strips of $\frac{1}{8}$-inch-wide white paper and cut six 4-inch pieces of wire. Straighten the wire and glue each piece between two white strips. Allow all pieces to dry. Set aside two of the strips for the long S scrolls on both sides. Cut the remaining 4-inch wire strips in the lengths needed. Make additional wire paper strips if needed.

3

Use the illustration for lengths and the specific shapes on the sides and ends. Shape the scrolls around dowels of all sizes. Trim the ends of the scrolls when they're completed. When dry, make any adjustments to ensure the bench is level and stands straight.

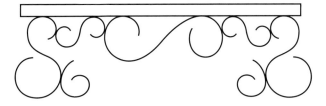

ASSEMBLY

1

To make the shadow box, use a rotary cutter to cut off all but a 2-inch-wide section of the white craft box's lid—this section will be covered with wavy-edged pinstriped paper to become the awning.

2

Measure, cut, and glue the pinstripe decorative paper inside the box. Then glue a $\frac{1}{4}$-inch strip of white paper inside around the lower portion of the inside walls to imitate a baseboard.

3

Cut a piece of pinstripe paper to cover the top and awning. Use the decorative-edge scissors to cut a wave at the bottom of the awning. Glue this in place.

4

To make the quilled flourish for the awning, start with the design in the center. Make a five-loop shape with a $1/8$ x $4 1/2$-inch white paper strip. Glue a 2-inch loose circle at the bottom of the loop shape. Make a 4-inch open heart shape and glue it around the bottom of the circle and loop shape (see the photo). Make a three-loop shape with a $1/8$ x 3-inch white paper strip (make two).

Make a V scroll using a 3-inch strip (make two). Make five 2-inch loose circles. Glue the V scrolls around the bottom of the loop shapes. Glue a 2-inch loose circle at the point of the V scrolls. Glue the two smaller three-loop shapes on both sides of the lower part of the five-loop shape. Glue the remaining three 2-inch loose circles at the lower center.

5

To make the matching designs on the sides of the flourish, first make two five-loop shapes from $1/8$ x $5 1/2$-inch white strips. Make two V scrolls using 4-inch strips. Roll two 2-inch loose circles. Glue the V scrolls around the bottom of the loop shapes. Glue a 2-inch loose circle at the point of each V scroll.

6

Using the photo as a guide, glue the flourish pieces in the center of the awning.

7

Arrange all the elements inside the shadow box.

DAZZLING PAISLEY MOBILE

These paisley motifs are fresh interpretations of a centuries-old design. Bright colors and the glittering touch of shiny sequins make them a dazzling addition to any room.

YOU WILL NEED

Basic quilling tool kit (page 8)

1/4-inch-wide paper strips
(various bright colors)

Paper crimper

1/8-inch dowel

Fine-tip glue bottle

Small, flat paintbrush

Sequins

Sewing needle

Monofilament

Mobile hanger or wind chime

BASIC TECHNIQUES USED

Loose circle (A)
Teardrop (B)
Paisley (C)

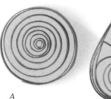

A   B   C

INSTRUCTIONS

NOTE▶• Each paisley hanging from the mobile is made up of two identical paisleys glued back to back with a strip of paper covering the seam. Chose three colors for each paisley (we used bright colors).

1

To achieve the tension needed, you'll quill the three colors for each paisley in three steps instead of gluing the different colored strips end-to-end and rolling them all at once. To begin, glue four 1/4 x 12-inch strips of one color end-to-end and run this through a paper crimper. Roll this into a loose circle. Place the circle on a flat surface and release to 1 1/4 inches in diameter. Glue the loose end to the side. This is the inner color.

2

Glue four 1/4 x 12-inch strips of another color end-to-end and run this through the paper crimper. This is the middle color. Glue one end to the glued seam on the loose circle and wrap the entire strip around and around the loose circle. Place the piece on a flat surface and release to 1 3/4 inches in diameter. Glue the loose end to the side.

3

Glue four more 1/4 x 12-inch strips of a third color end-to-end and run this through the paper crimper. This is the outer color. Glue one end to the glued seam on the above loose circle and wrap the entire strip around and around the loose circle. Lay the loose circle on a flat surface and release the tension to 2 1/4 inches in diameter. Glue down the loose end.

4

Shape the piece into a paisley by first making a teardrop. Pinch in about two-thirds of the way down from the wide end of the teardrop, slightly flatten the remaining third, and curl the pointed end on the-inch dowel.

5

Repeat steps 1 through 4 to make an identical paisley.

6

Before you glue two matching paisleys together, you need to apply a glue-backing to each of them. (See page 27 for more on the glue-backing technique.) To apply a glue-backing, first place the two paisley shapes under a sheet of acetate, top-side-up, with the curled ends facing opposite directions—make sure they're placed under the acetate and pointing in opposite directions!

7

Use the fine-tip glue bottle to begin outlining the paisley shapes on the top of the acetate. Use the paintbrush to fill in the outline with glue. Remove the two paisley shapes from under the acetate and place them on top of the glue. If the tension in the centers is loose or not uniform, use tweezers to hold the center and rotate the tweezers in the direction of the coil to make the tension tighter and more consistent. (This will be important when you try to attach the sequins.)

8

Peel the paisleys from the acetate when the glue is clear and dry. Apply a small amount of glue to the glued side of one piece and glue the two paisleys together, glued side to glued side. Tear a 9-inch-long strip of the outer color paper. Run it through the paper crimper. Make a small hole in the center of the crimped strip with a needle. Knot one end of an 18-inch length of monofilament and thread it through the hole. Glue the strip around the joined edge of the two glued paisley shapes to hide the seam and to cover up any uneven edges.

9

Glue sequins on one side or both to outline or fill in the inner paisley shape. Let dry.

10

Hang the paisleys to the wind chime, adjusting the length of the monofilament to balance the shapes.

TIP▶ • **You may make your own mobile, but it's easier to purchase a wind chime at a discount store, remove the chimes, and replace them with the quilled paisleys.**

WEDDING DOVES TABLE SETTING

Quilling can add a handcrafted touch to a wedding. A graceful dove motif can be added to any number of small projects to make your wedding unique—on favor boxes, place cards, candy wrappers, napkin rings, and whatever captures your fancy.

YOU WILL NEED

Basic quilling tool kit (page 8)

1/8- and 3/4-inch-wide medium-weight

paper strips (ivory)

Hand punch, 3/8-inch fern

Half-pearls

Border punch

Gold vellum

Cake box template (page 118)

Photocopier or tracing paper

Card stock, beige

Paper trimmer

BASIC TECHNIQUES USED

Loose circle (A)

Shaped marquise (B)

Punched leaf

S scroll (optional) (C)

Punched border

Double quilling

Teardrop (D)

Tendril (E)

INSTRUCTIONS

1

To make a dove, first roll a $1/8$ x 14-inch strip of ivory paper into a loose circle $7/8$ inch in diameter. Pinch this into a shaped marquise for the body. Make two shaped marquises using $1/8$ x 5-inch and $1/8$ x 7-inch strips of ivory paper for the wings. Glue the wings on the body, referring to the photo for placement.

2

Add a punched paper branch under the front point of the dove, and add a half-pearl to the top of the branch. We used a fern leaf for the branch; however, you can use a punch for an ash leaf or glue a 1-inch S scroll to the tip of the dove instead.

A

3

To add the decorative border to items, measure the circumference of the item you're decorating and cut $3/4$-inch-wide strips of ivory paper to that length. Glue strips end-to-end if needed for the lengths required. Use the border punch to punch across the $3/4$-inch-wide ivory strip, but don't punch the first or last inch of the strip.

B

4

Place the decorative strip over a $5/8$-inch-wide strip of gold vellum and glue it at one end. Wrap the punched paper and gold vellum strip around the item to be decorated. Glue the other end of the vellum down first, pull the decorative strip tight over it, and glue it down (the ends of the strips should overlap slightly).

C

5

Photocopy or trace the cake box template on page 118 and follow the template directions to make the box from the beige card stock. Follow the instructions in steps 3 and 4 to embellish the sides of the box. Punch a single strip of $3/4$ x 2 $3/4$-inch ivory paper and attach it to the back of box.

D

6

Make a bow for the square favor box by using two $3/4$ x 8 $1/4$-inch strips of punched ivory paper glued (at one end) over two $5/8$ x 8-$1/2$-inch strips

E

of gold vellum. (See page 24 for instructions for double quilling and page 39 for making a formal bow.) Begin rolling at the glued end and make a loose circle 1 inch in diameter. Repeat to make the other loose circle.

7

Pull the centers toward the glued seam with tweezers and pinch to make teardrop shapes. Glue the two points together and allow to dry. Make the center roll with a strip of $3/4$ x 4-inch punched ivory paper over a $5/8$ x 4-inch strip of gold vellum. Make a loose circle $3/8$ inch in diameter. Glue it on top between the two sides, as shown in the photo.

8

To make a napkin ring, glue two $3/4$ x 12-inch strips of ivory paper end-to-end and fold evenly twice to make a 6-inch-long strip. Cut through the sides at the ends as shown in the illustration on page 118. Wrap around a folded napkin and fit the ends together at the slits. Add a quilled design to the top.

TIP • Use a combination of soft ivory and ivory shades for a sophisticated look. Other motifs to use for a wedding tablescape are quilled hearts, initials, fringed flowers, quilled petal flowers, or a flourish.

ELEGANTLY EMBELLISHED KEEPSAKE

Give the happy couple (or the beleaguered parents and in-laws) a unique, personalized gift to mark the special day. Add quilled elements in the wedding colors or opt for the elegance of neutral tones.

Mr. and Mrs. John David Smith
request the honor of your presence
at the marriage of their daughter

Mary Lynn

to

Mr. William Richard Jones

on Saturday, the third of June

at three o'clock in the afternoon

United Methodist Church

Fort Worth, Texas

YOU WILL NEED

Basic quilling tool kit (page 8)

1/8-inch-wide paper strips (soft ivory)

1³/₄ inch dowel

Wedding invitation

Plain paper, 8 x 10 inches

Matted frame, 8 x 10 inches

BASIC TECHNIQUES USED

Open heart (A)

Tendril (B)

Folded Rose (C)

Marquise (D)

Shaped marquise (E)

S scroll (F)

Loose scroll (G)

Note: Choose a frame and mat that will complement the invitation and reflect the style of the couple. An ivory mat with a 5 x 7-inch opening is used here. Choose the size and colors that will work best with your particular invitation.

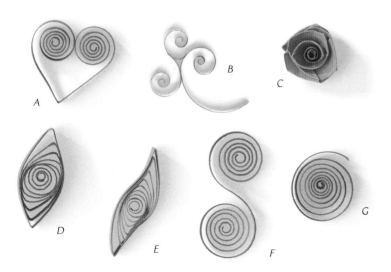

INSTRUCTIONS

1

Make and arrange all shapes prior to gluing. Make more shapes than needed so you can choose the best ones to use. To make the two open hearts, use 3¹/₄- and 4¹/₄-inch-long paper strips. Fold each ¹/₄ inch off-center prior to rolling the ends. Make tendrils from the coils, and then shape the hearts as shown in the photo.

2

Make folded roses(see page 20) using 3¹/₂- and 4 inch-long paper strips.

3

To make the leaves, make marquises and shaped marquises from 2¹/₂-, 3-, and 4-inch-long paper strips.

4

Use two 1³/₄-inch-long strips to make the rings. To make perfectly round rings and create the effect of interlocking bands, it's necessary to make two rings and then cut one into two pieces. To begin, wrap one strip around the dowel. Overlap the ends and glue. Repeat with the second strip. Let the glue completely dry on both rings. Using the photo as a guide, cut a small section off one ring. Glue this section inside the uncut ring. Glue the rest of the cut ring up against the outside of the uncut ring, making sure to perfectly match up the four cut ends.

5

Make S scrolls using 2-, 3-, and 4-inch-long paper strips. Make tendrils with the coils.

6

Make loose scrolls using 1½- and 2-inch paper strips. Make tendrils with the coils.

7

Arrange the shapes on the invitation using the photo as a guide. Glue the quilled pieces to the invitation using only small dots of glue. Allow to dry, then center the completed invitation on the sheet of plain paper. Place the mat over the invitation and insert it into the frame.

TIP▶ • Use this type of design to frame special cards, scrapbook pages, or anniversary announcements.

KEEPSAKE TRIO

This trio of quilled boxes can hold precious keepsakes and small treasures. These boxes are easy to make—you select the box size and the complexity of your embellishment. Even if you make only one, the end result will be a keeper!

YOU WILL NEED

Basic quilling tool kit (page 8)

Papier-mâché boxes

¹/₄- and ¹/₈-inch-wide paper strips (ivory)

Paintbrush

Acrylic paint, ivory (glossy or matte finish)

Decoupage scissors (or fringing tool)

Chalk (color of your choice)

Acid-free spray fixative

Note: Papier-mâché boxes are available in all shapes and sizes. Paint the boxes with two coats of acrylic paint.

BASIC TECHNIQUES USED

Chalking (page 25)

Small bullet (A)

Tight circle (peg) (B)

Loose circle (C)

Shaped marquise (D)

Looped leaf (E)

Folded rose (F)

Fringed flower with center (G)

S scroll (H)

Open heart (I)

Teardrop (J)

Marquise (K)

Fringed flower (L)

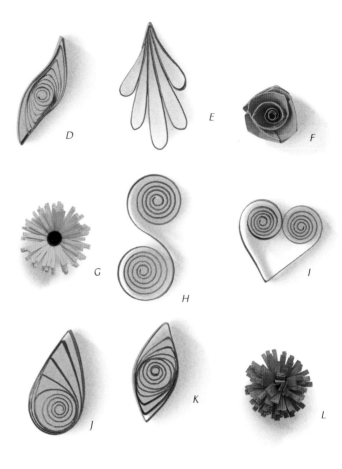

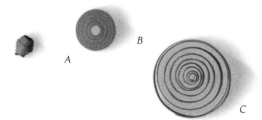

INSTRUCTIONS LARGE BOX

1

Make all of the following quilled shapes for the large oval box. All paper used is ¹/₈-inch wide except where indicated. Use the same color or shades of the box color for an elegant monochromatic effect.

Make 16 bullets from eight 1-inch strips (for flower centers and step 2).

Make six tight circles from three 1-inch strips; make nine from 2-inch strips (for flower centers and pegs).

Make six loose circles from 2-inch strips (for pegs).

Make three shaped marquises from 4-inch strips; make two from 3-inch strips (for leaves).

Make two looped leaves from 5-inch strips; make one from a 4-inch strip.

Make three folded roses using 1/4 x 5-inch strips.

Make three fringed flowers with centers using 1/4 x 3-inch fringed strips, 1/8 x 2-inch strips for centers, and a bullet glued on top of each center.

Make three S scrolls using 2-inch strips.

Make one open heart using a 2-inch strip.

2

Cut a sliver of paper to 1/16 x 1 1/2 inches and glue a bullet shape to the end. Glue a second bullet 1/4 inch below on the opposite side. Glue four more bullets down the strip, alternating sides.

3

Make the following five-petal flowers: one with five teardrops using 2-inch strips, one with five teardrops using 2 1/2-inch strips, and one with five teardrops using 3-inch strips. Make three tight circles using 2-inch strips for the centers.

4

Make the following six-petal flowers of different sizes: one with six marquises using 2-inch strips, one with six marquises using 2 1/2-inch strips, and one with six marquises using 3-inch strips. Make three tight circles using 2-inch strips for the centers (bullets can be used for flower centers in lieu of tight circles).

SMALL BOXES

Fewer pieces are needed for the smaller boxes unless you want to cover the entire box lid.

1

Make two fringed flowers using 1/4 x 4-inch fringed strips, and make one fringed flower with center using a 1/4 x 3-inch fringed strip.

2

Make three small looped leaves using 4-inch strips.

3

Make small roses using 1/8 x 4-inch strips.

4

Make enough S scrolls to go around the edge of the lid, creating a filigree border.

ASSEMBLY

Glue pegs under the largest flowers to give them dimension. Start gluing shapes in the center of the lid and work out and around, using the photo as a guide to place various shapes. Apply glue to the ends of leaves and tuck them under the elevated flowers.

Wait until the glue has dried completely before adding chalked highlights to the flowers (see page 25). Use a color for contrast or brown/black for an antique effect. Turn the lid over carefully to let excess chalk fall off, then lightly spray the finished piece with the fixative to prevent smudging.

TIP▶● Store any unused shapes in a box. When you have enough leftover shapes, make a small trinket box. Mixing colors for your quilled shapes will produce a totally different appearance.

TEMPLATES

Trés Chic Trio of Dresses (page 83)

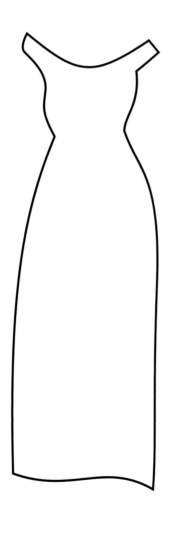

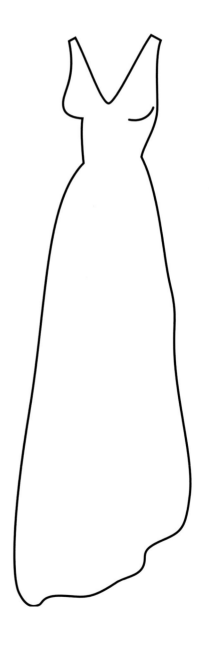

Funky Faux Flower Leaf *(page 70)*

Napkin Ring (*page 106*)

Cake Box (*page 106*)

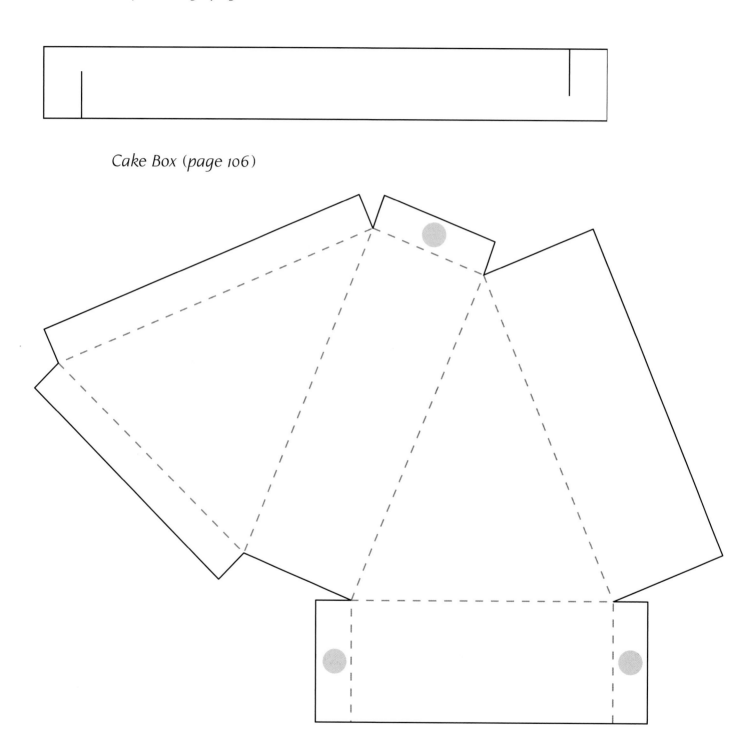

Quilled Circle Alphabet (*page 66*)

Filliped Alphabet (page 62)

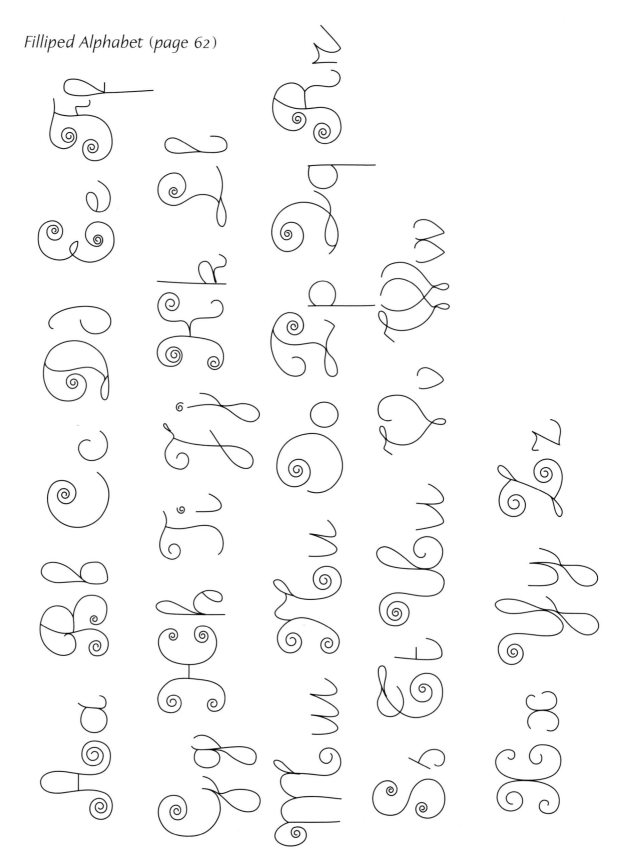

Graceful Script Alphabet (page 58)

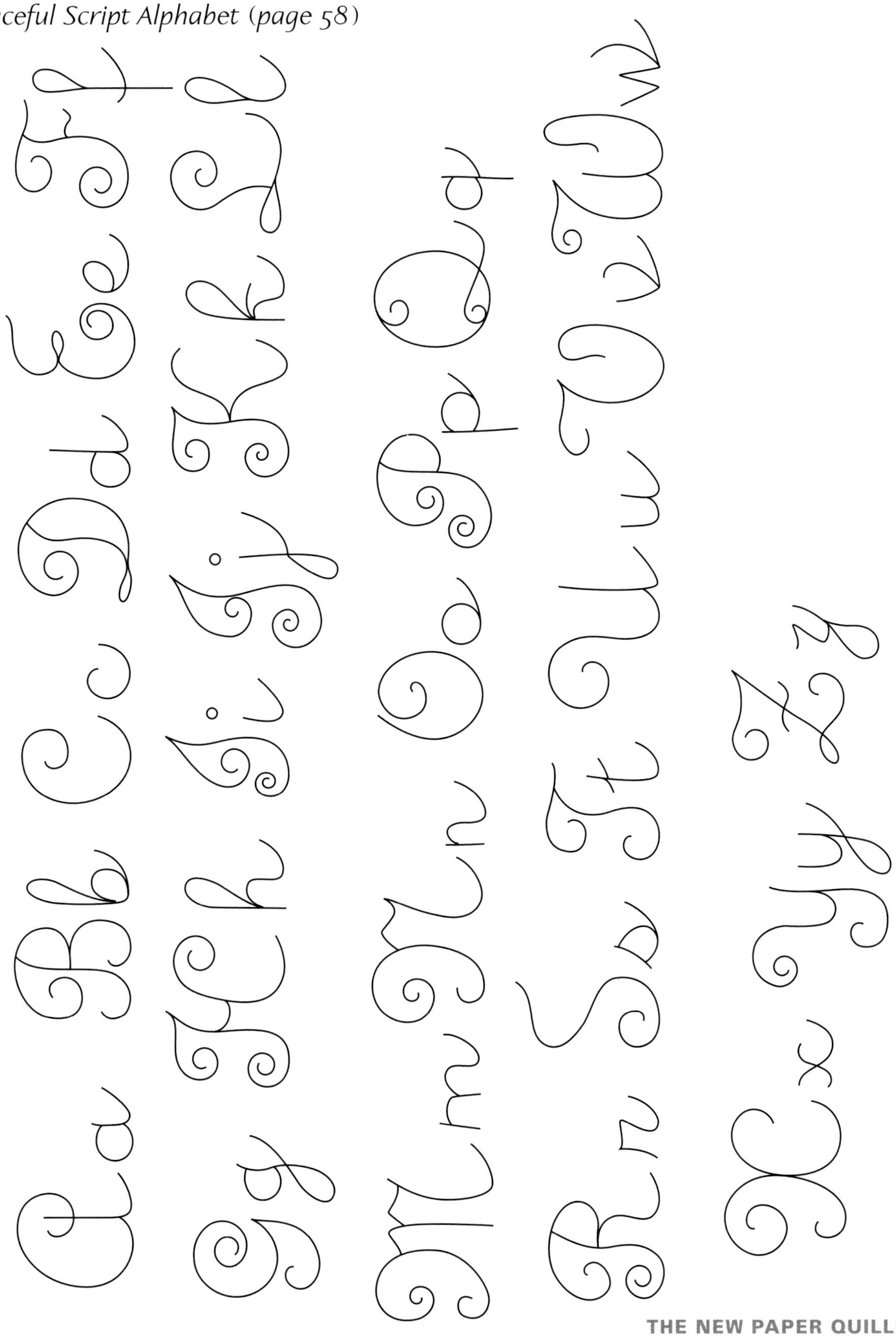

Aa Bb Cc Dd Ee Ff

Gg Hh Ii Jj Kk Ll

Mm Nn Oo Pp Qq

Rr Ss Tt Uu Vv Ww

Xx Yy Zz

Longevity Seal (*page 78*)　　　　　　　　　　*Sunny Sunflower Wreath* (*page 50*)

Work Board, enlarge 133%

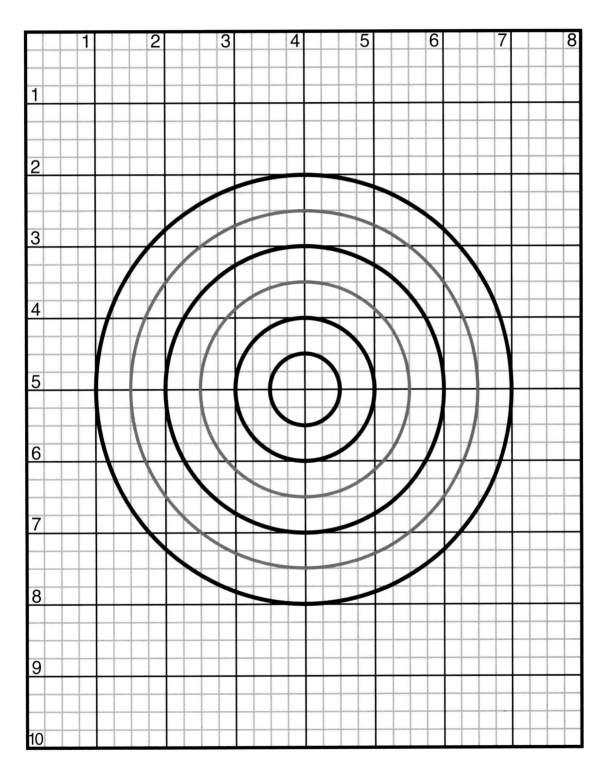

METRIC CONVERSION CHART

Inches	Millimeters (mm)/ Centimeters (cm)	Inches	Millimeters (mm)/ Centimeters (cm)	Inches	Millimeters (mm)/ Centimeters (cm)
1/8	3 mm	8	20.3 cm	22 1/2	57.2 cm
3/16	5 mm	8 1/2	21.6 cm	23	58.4 cm
1/4	6 mm	9	22.9 cm	23 1/2	59.7 cm
5/16	8 mm	9 1/2	24.1 cm	24	61 cm
3/8	9.5 mm	10	25.4 cm	24 1/2	62.2 cm
7/16	1.1 cm	10 1/2	26.7 cm	25	63.5 cm
1/2	1.3 cm	11	27.9 cm	25 1/2	64.8 cm
9/16	1.4 cm	11 1/2	29.2 cm	26	66 cm
5/8	1.6 cm	12	30.5 cm	26 1/2	67.3 cm
11/16	1.7 cm	12 1/2	31.8 cm	27	68.6 cm
3/4	1.9 cm	13	33 cm	27 1/2	69.9 cm
13/16	2.1 cm	13 1/2	34.3 cm	28	71.1 cm
7/8	2.2 cm	14	35.6 cm	28 1/2	72.4 cm
15/16	2.4 cm	14 1/2	36.8 cm	29	73.7 cm
		15	38.1 cm	29 1/2	74.9 cm
1	2.5 cm	15 1/2	39.4 cm	30	76.2 cm
1 1/2	3.8 cm	16	40.6 cm	30 1/2	77.5 cm
2	5 cm	16 1/2	41.9 cm	31	78.7 cm
2 1/2	6.4 cm	17	43.2 cm	31 1/2	80 cm
3	7.6 cm	17 1/2	44.5 cm	32	81.3 cm
3 1/2	8.9 cm	18	45.7 cm	32 1/2	82.6 cm
4	10.2 cm	18 1/2	47 cm	33	83.8 cm
4 1/2	11.4 cm	19	48.3 cm	33 1/2	85 cm
5	12.7 cm	19 1/2	49.5 cm	34	86.4 cm
5 1/2	14 cm	20	50.8 cm	34 1/2	87.6 cm
6	15.2 cm	20 1/2	52 cm	35	88.9 cm
6 1/2	16.5 cm	21	53.3	35 1/2	90.2 cm
7	17.8 cm	21 1/2	54.6	36	91.4 cm
7 1/2	19 cm	22	55 cm		

INDEX

ACKNOWLEDGMENTS

Thanks to my caring family—Mother and Daddy, Aunt Maxine, Horace, Rob, Joshua, Kay, Ron, Rhonda, Taylor, Bobby, Amy, and Baylee—for enduring my absence at gatherings, my constant complaints, and mumbled jargon about deadlines. You all inspire and encourage me, in addition to being my biggest promoters.

Thanks to my loving daughter and advisor, Renay, who gives me constant reassurance and keeps me balanced through bouts of adversity. Also to Bryan, Blake, and Brandon for just making me smile and being there.

Thanks to my husband Chris who frequently played golf to give me the time and solitude to complete the projects and write this book. Thank you for your sacrifice (ha!) and never-ending support and love.

For their years of dedication in the quilling industry, I have enormous respect for Malinda and Jim Johnston.

For their unconditional support, my quilling designer and friend, Eileen, and my designer-mentor, Patt.

Thanks to all the amazing people at Lark Books—art directors, photographers, and illustrators—who work until they get things done right. I sincerely appreciate your hard work.

Thanks to Deborah Morgenthal who opened the door at Lark and let me walk through. Without her vision and determination, this book would still to be a mass of data and ideas in my mind. Kathy Sheldon identified all my faux pas and magically changed my writing into easy-to-understand text. And, for his expertise, artistic insight, timely humor, commitment, and superb time-management, I want to thank my fabulous project coordinator and editor, Terry Taylor. This is nearly as much his book as it is mine.

DEDICATION

To the memory of my beloved sisters, Linda and Cindy.